Our Caribbean and Global Insecurity

Printed in the United States

This is the third volume in a series entitled
Caribbean Ideas
published by Strategy Forum, Inc.
Kingstown, St. Vincent and the Grenadines

Other titles in the series include
Our Caribbean Civilisation and Its Political Prospects
The Case for Caribbean Reparatory Justice

Our Caribbean and Global Insecurity

Seven Essays by
Dr The Hon. Ralph E. Gonsalves
Prime Minister of St. Vincent & the Grenadines

Table of Contents

Preface

In the prologue to *The Making of the Comrade, the Political Journey of Ralph Gonsalves*, Professor Sir Hilary Beckles, vice chancellor of the University of the West Indies, said "No one, since Dr Eric Williams, has departed the academy and delved so deeply into the polity, and with such haste and good taste" as Comrade Ralph has in our Caribbean context. This collection of seven lectures, entitled *Our Caribbean and Global Insecurity*, is the third in the Caribbean Ideas series. Like the collections that preceded it, this one points beyond the political acumen and leadership of Dr Gonsalves and reminds us that he remains ever the intellectual and teacher and, above all, underscores the indelible fact that he is a quintessential Caribbean man.

This volume begins with a lecture entitled "Sovereignty, Independence and Intellectual Thought in the Caribbean: The Legacy of Gordon R. Lewis", which, incidentally, was part of a previous collection entitled *Our Caribbean Civilisation and Its Political Prospects*. This lecture appropriately anchors the broad theme of *Our Caribbean and Global Insecurity*. The opening sentence, "Today, our Caribbean is engaged in a profound search for a way out of its enveloping socio-economic and political challenges not experienced since independence..." establishes the thesis of this volume. The lectures span the period May 2009 through June 2016 and take us on a journey of reflections on the life, thought and contribution of Caribbean leaders like Maurice Bishop of Grenada, Errol Barrow of Barbados and Cheddi Jagan of Guyana. Such reflections are not complete without the inclusion of the Caribbean perspective on theology and the church and their role in shaping the political landscape, which is the subject of the fifth lecture herein. Here too, Dr Gonsalves places our Caribbean perspective in a global context.

The Caribbean's role in paving the way for the US–Cuba Accord is the penultimate lecture collected within. This lecture, the 17th Eric E. WIlliams Memorial Lecture, was delivered on October 23, 2015, at the Florida International University before a packed hall of hundreds. I was honoured to be among those present, privileged to witness the standing ovation of the audience, proud to be a citizen of a small island state whose prime minister can command the respect and admiration of an international audience of the calibre that was in attendance that evening. This penultimate lecture, beyond its pertinence to the theme of this collection, registers the history of the late great Caribbean leader, Fidel Castro, within a CARICOM context and lays a foundation for the unfolding of the normalisation and restoration of the US–Cuba relations. It further demonstrates how four titans of the Caribbean namely, Eric Williams of Trinidad and Tobago, Michael Manley of Jamaica, Errol Barrow of Barbados, and Forbes Burnham of Guyana (and the author of this preface believes Dr Gonsalves is worthy of inclusion in this list) paved the way for this important accord.

The title of the book is taken from the last lecture in this collection. "Global Insecurity" was presented to the University College of the Cayman Islands in June 2016. Its enquiry, according to Dr Gonsalves, is "historical, contemporary and comparative" and endeavors to contemplate "[the] critical question of what level of global insecurity is tolerable and consistent with a level of living that accords with the accepted standards of human civilisation." He further asserts that

Global insecurity arises from multiple sources. Among the principle sources are: Contradictions and crises of global capitalism and other extant economic arrangements; economic dominance and resistance; inequality and poverty; adverse climate change and its consequences; the spread of nuclear weapons and the arms race generally; the pursuit of power grounded in ideology; the quest for hegemony based on religion; the turmoil in governance arrangements in several countries...

The list continues and does suggest that contemplation of this issue is timely. November 8, 2016, saw the unprecedented win of Donald J. Trump who was inaugurated on January 20, 2017, as the 45th President of the United States of America. Wherever one finds oneself on the expectation spectrum, everyone agrees we have entered new and interesting times. As I pen this preface, after hours at my desk at the Permanent Mission of Saint Vincent and the Grenadines to the United Nations, I learn of President Trump's intention to sign executive orders that will "drastically reduce the U.S. role in the United Nations and other international organisations", according to the *New York Times*. *Our Caribbean and Global Insecurity* is, therefore, an important collection and a necessary read. It creates a critical reference point as we navigate the changing contours of a new world dynamic.

Inga Rhonda King
New York
January 2017

Sovereignty, Independence and Intellectual Thought in the Caribbean: The Legacy of Gordon R. Lewis

(Address delivered at the Gordon Lewis Symposium, University of the West Indies, Mona, Jamaica, December 1, 2010.)

Today, our Caribbean is engaged in a profound search for a way out of its enveloping socio-economic and political challenges of a magnitude not experienced since independence. This symposium on the intellectual work of Gordon R. Lewis and its impact on political thought in our region is bound to assist. This Welshman's encounter with our Caribbean has produced intellectual insights and political analysis of both context and text that have shone with a brightness that illuminates and does not blind. He has caused us to reflect on overarching themes grounded in an admixture of geography, culture, political sociology, the literature of the creative imagination, political economy, and political praxis, with a freshness and creativity that are now more needed than ever.

All this jumps out at us as Gordon Lewis traverses the growth of the modern West Indies, the intellectual and ideational foundations of our Caribbean, the independence of Puerto Rico and our Caribbean, the despoiling of the jewel that was revolutionary Grenada, and the integration and political sociology of our multi-languaged region.

Like the Barbadian and Caribbean poet, H. A. Vaughn, in his minor classic "Revelation", Gordon Lewis saw the Caribbean and its people as manifestations of a beauty that escaped colonial schools. As such Lewis railed against those who caused us to "keep tight lips for burnished beauty nearer home" and who urged us to prate, to extol as ideal that which came from Greece, Rome, and "the face that launched a thousand ships". This elemental and uplifting embrace by Lewis of the intrinsic magnificence of our people stands in contrast to some who have come from the metaphoric "niggeryard of yesterday" with the scorn of themselves arising, seemingly paradoxically, from the oppressor's hate. Like Martin Carter of Guyana, Lewis saw the consciousness of our being as our central strength for our challenging tomorrows. To be sure, Gordon Lewis acknowledged and explored sharply our region's limitations and weaknesses but he always returned to our strengths and possibilities. Truth is beauty, too. This dialectical thought process never allowed him to descend into a trendy learned helplessness of prelates, political poseurs and the pontiffs of a manufactured consensus emanating from international financial institutions. Lewis was always positive, upbeat and optimistic about our region's possibilities.

Recently, I was reading some essays authored by the Franco-Czech novelist, Milan Kundera, and published in 2009 under the title, *Encounter*. It struck me that he was onto a Lewis theme while he was discussing Aimé Cesaire, Patrick Chamoiseau and Martinique. Kundera was seeking to locate a margin, which every people searches for, between its own home and the world. This margin or realm between national and global contexts Kundera calls "the median context". For example, a Chilean has Latin America as its median context; a Swede has its Scandavia bloc. But some countries such as Austria, Greece and Turkey have difficulty identifying their median context. Kundera advises that:

There are some nations whose identity is characterized by duality, by the complexity of their median context, and that's precisely what gives them their particularity.

As to Martinique, I would say the same thing: the coexistence of various different median contexts there is what makes for the particularity of its culture. Martinique: a multiple intersection; a crosswords among the continents; a tiny slip of land where France, Africa, the Americas meet.

Yes, that's beautiful. Very beautiful, except that France, Africa, America don't care much. In today's world that voice of small entities is barely heard.

Martinique: the encounter of a great cultural complexity with a great solitude.

Incidentally, for those who contest this lack of caring or hearing by the metropolises for, and of, the Caribbean, may learn otherwise if they consult the biography of Bill Clinton entitled *My Life* (2004) and that of Tony Blair, *A Journey* (2010). Those two western leaders of "the third way" mentioned the Caribbean only fleetingly. In neither biography did the mention warrant inclusion in the comprehensive index. The Caribbean was simply ignored.

Gordon Lewis was partly consumed in seeking to understand the "great cultural complexity" called the Caribbean, its impact on our region's society, economy and polity, and its median context or destiny in a united or integrated Caribbean amidst the solitude of island nationalisms or even chauvinisms. How to bring together, optimally in a coherent unit, the Caribbean islands and territories each awash with it peculiarities but all conjoined by overwhelming commonalities, remains an enduring problematic.

Gordon Lewis accepted almost entirely the analysis and prescription for an integrated Caribbean of his friend, Dr Eric Williams, the legendary historian and political leader from Trinidad and Tobago. Lewis saw the collapse of the West Indian federal venture of the early 1960s not so much as the consequence of bickering political personalities or disruptive island nationalisms but as fundamentally a failure of conception. For him, the weak apparatus, constitutionally, of the central government in the Federation was a colonial construct derived from a classical notion of a federation but which in the Caribbean amounted to an unworkable confederation. His preference was for a much stronger central government as envisaged in Williams' *Economics of Nationhood*. It is to be seriously doubted, however, that such a model would have survived the political marketplace. It would be a simplistic error to conclude, as Lewis did not, that a "secessionist" Jamaica was or is the only bull in the regional china shop. In the early 1990s, Sir James Mitchell, Prime Minister of St. Vincent and the Grenadines, found out that his advocacy of a "unitary state" or at least a "strong federal centre" for a Windwards-Leewards Political Union was shot down as pie-in-the-sky dreaming.

We are all still absorbed with this issue of regional governance in an integrated Caribbean. The Grand Anse Declaration of 1989, the Revised Treaty of Chaguaramas of 2001, the Rose Hall Declaration of 2003, the Gonsalves-led Prime Ministerial Working Group of 2003 to 2007, the Vaughn Lewis Technical Working Group of 2007, and the recent Montego Bay Decision of 2010 are all staging posts in the journey to resolve the intractable governance conundrum in the Caribbean Community (CARICOM). The Economic Union Treaty of the Organisation of Eastern Caribbean States (OECS) of 2010 takes the practical pursuit of a governance solution along the continuum away from confederalism but not yet to a full federal exercise. The jury is still out on its efficacy, although its future is promising.

Interestingly, Gordon Lewis's starting point for his penetrating analysis of the Caribbean begins with his profound appreciation of nature's impact. It is an obvious fact but so easily missed by some other accomplished commentators. The first sentence in his magisterial analysis published in 1968 and known to us as *The Growth of the Modern West Indies*, is quite arresting:

> The most striking single feature of the Caribbean chains of the West Indies society is, perhaps, their unique geographical position.

It is almost akin to the first line, too, in Roy Strong's 1966 volume, *History of Britain*: "Britain is an island and that fact is more important than any other in understanding its history".

This "most striking single feature" of the Caribbean's "unique geographical position" encompasses its location, the spread of the archipelago, its geology, its landscape and seascape, and its climate. But for Lewis, nature is the starting point, not the end point. So, he tells us:

> The real oppressions of West Indian life, however, have not been so much those of nature and geography as those of history and culture. If the region has been since slavery Emancipation (1834) nothing much more than a geographical expression, that had been due in the main part, to the legacy of its colonial history in all of its manifold forms. It is nurture, not nature, that has produced from the historical beginnings, that Balkanisation of the regional government and politics. The real barriers have been the artificial ones, linguistic, monetary, commercial, for the mutual ignorance and sometimes mutual hostilities of the various island populations, even when they are all English-speaking, stem from the fact that colonisation decreed that the avenues of

communication should be between each individual West Indian fief and London, rather than between the territories themselves.

...Political imperialism, in brief, explains more than any other single factor, the present disunity of the region, the aimlessness so distressingly apparent since the collapse of the federal venture in 1962, with the resultant trend towards micro-nationalism. Cultural imperialism, in its turn, by seeking through education to convert the West Indian person into a coloured English gentleman produced the contemporary spectacle of the West Indian as a culturally disinherited individual, an Anglicised colonial set with an Afro-Asian cultural environment, caught between the dying Anglophile world and the new world of Caribbean democracy and nationalism seeking to be born.

This bundle of criss-crossing issues, their historical and sociological underpinnings, their political expressions, and the people's quest for sovereignty, democracy, and an enhanced condition of living, are what preoccupied Gordon Lewis on his extended and productive Caribbean sojourn. As he had put it himself, his prolonged residence in the Caribbean area, along with his strategically-located perch in Puerto Rico, had given him "the right to be heard". And we are hearing him clearly.

Lewis had a scientist's instinctive aversion to facile, simplistic and over-stretched formalistic explanations to the real condition of the Caribbean. To be sure, he was curious and intellectually adventurous but he never allowed his curiosity and adventurousness to take him to fanciful flights from what was closest and most concrete. Much of the celebrated writings by too many intellectuals in our region and elsewhere stray too easily from scientific observation and analysis of the actual condition of life in society. On this we can all learn from Lewis.

Indeed, this subject is an enduring one in intellectual thought. In a remarkable book entitled *The Conscience of Words and Earwitness*, published in 1987, the distinguished European Nobel Laureate for Literature, Elias Canetti, had this to say:

> Among the most sinister phenomena in intellectual history is the avoidance of the concrete. People have had a conscious tendency to go first after the most remote things, ignoring everything they stumble over close by. The élan of outgoing gestures, the boldness and adventure of expeditions to faraway places camouflage their motives. The not infrequent goal is to avoid what lies near because we are not up to it.... But the situation of mankind today, as we all know, is so serious that we have to turn to what is closest and most concrete.

Much of political science literature in the Caribbean, before and after Gordon Lewis, has been pre-occupied with legal-institutional analysis, the poring over of survey data of this or that opinion poll, impressionist behavioural studies, the political sparring between competing elites, and over-playing the importance to political understanding of "charisma" or "hero-crowd" conceptions. It is not that these do not form part of the analytic mix which leads towards a comprehensive theory of explanation, but as stand-alone offerings they become momentary, ahistorical snap-shots rather than a thorough-going explanation.

Let us illustrate all this with Lewis' robust rebuke of Archibald W. Singham, the well-known Sinhalese political scientist who lived and toiled lovingly among us for many years, on the issue of charismatic leadership as an explanatory frame for Caribbean politics. Singham was to elaborate his thesis in his celebrated volume entitled *The Hero and the Crowd in a Colonial Polity*, published by Yale University Press in 1967. Lewis is unlikely to have read Singham's book before his *Growth of the Modern West Indies* went to press, but he had certainly read the Singham thesis in the latter's mimeographed paper entitled "Political Crisis and Electoral Change in a Colonial Society" which was presented at the 1963 annual meeting of the American Political Science Association.

In referencing Singham's 1963 paper, Lewis joined the battle in the following terms:

> The cause célèbre of the battle in the Windwards was, of course, the phenomenal rise of Gairy and Gairyism after 1950. A West Indian political scientist (meaning Singham) has attempted to see the movement in Weberian terms. But it is doubtful if a schematic analysis that sees Gairy as the Weberian charismatic leader and the Grenada Government as the embodiment of rationalistic bureaucracy does anything more than describe the institutional superstructure while ignoring, except for a brief description, the social class struggle out of which Gairyism emerged; not to mention the fact that the procedure attributes motivational factors to the actors of the drama and seriously distorts the meaning of what actually happened. For "charisma" is not a self-generating first cause; it grows out of deep social crisis. Gairy's providential return to Grenada in 1946 from the Aruba oil fields – the nursery of West Indian agitational leadership – did not create the crisis. It merely provided the crisis with its appropriate leadership. To be properly understood, it must be seen in terms of (1) its socio-cultural environment and (2) the old-style Grenadian political leadership that preceded it.

This is compelling and persuasive stuff. But it is clear that Lewis is not Marxian in that he subscribes simply to "social classes" as the sole explanatory fulcrum or that "social class struggle", simpliciter, is the motor force of history. It is true that Lewis searches for explanations embedded in the social and historical condition which gave rise to Gairy and Gairyism but that involves a host of factors, a veritable parallelogram of forces, including class, race, culture, colonialism, the crisis of underdevelopment, the people's aspirations, class struggles, and the peculiarities of particular leaderships. These Lewis combines into a whole, which he observes in their dialectical inter-connections over historical time.

In the process, Lewis contributes to our creative, unfettered thinking, but linked always to our real condition and our quest for a better life as a sovereign people. I thus recommend to all a re-read of Lewis' final chapter in *The Growth of the Modern West Indies* entitled "The Challenge of Independence" and his "Notes on the Puerto Rican Revolution", published in 1974.

Gordon Lewis was absolutely sure that "independence means a national stock-taking of heroic proportions". No institution is to be spared review, renewal, appropriate alteration, or re-creation. The political party, the trade union, the church, and the formal institutions of government were, in his view, to be subject to overhaul, restructuring, enhancement. This correct prescription is still to shape an urgent agenda at hand; at best, it is still a work-in-progress with a long way to go.

Moreover, Lewis is compelling in what he considers to be among the central challenges of independence. He rightly opines:

> It is not enough, with independence, to be merely against something, however justifiably. One must be for something. The social energies of newly liberated peoples, hitherto underutilised in the colonial system, now await the invention of new institutions and new purposes to fulfill themselves. The West Indies, after some early false starts, are thus clearly on the move. The basic questions of their future revolve not around the movement itself, but around the direction in which it will propel itself.

Independence, for Lewis, means, too, "a new positive citizenship". According to him:

> A new type of public opinion must be organised as the popular base of that citizenship. Equally, a new sense of personal responsibility, of personal involvement, must grow up, for much of what passes for new national spirit is frequently a sterile anti-colonial prejudice.

This call for personal responsibility and collective ownership of the society and political process resonates with all of us who champion enhanced good governance in this part of our Earthly City. This "personal responsibility" and "collective ownership" are vital cornerstones for the further ennoblement of our Caribbean civilisation and its institutional, political expressions.

In the case of Puerto Rico, Lewis was passionate about Puerto Rico becoming an independent, socialist, and democratic republic. In his "Notes on the Puerto Rican Revolution", he thundered, as a public and activist intellectual:

> The final argument for independence...is that it will finally release the hitherto suppressed moral and spiritual energies of the Puerto Rican people in the service of a new society based on the maxim of equality. These energies have hitherto been curtailed and limited by authoritarian and elitist structures of government.... Only a thorough destruction of that system can make way for popular, day-to-day political participation and industrial and agricultural self-government on the part of the workers. Only then can the remarkable moral and social qualities of the Puerto Rican people...receive their full expression.

Given Lewis' anti-colonial, anti-imperialist, socialist-oriented, and regionalist stance, it was painful for him and all those of like mind to experience, even at a distance, the heartache and sorrow of the collapse of the Grenada Revolution in October 1983 and the almost concurrent invasion by the United States of America. His rendering of this sad period of our history and politics is worth re-reading, too. The consequences still reverberate.

In my autobiographical volume entitled *The Making of "The Comrade": The Political Journey of Ralph Gonsalves*, I have written on this subject, in part, as follows:

> The death of the Grenada Revolution opened up the way for the triumph of reactionary and backward forces in the Caribbean under the imperial hegemony of Ronald Reagan's USA and Margaret Thatcher's Britain. Creative intellectual thought in the region was stifled as the Washington consensus fashioned by the International Monetary Fund (IMF) and the World Bank took root in our universities, regional institutions, major political parties, the mass media, and the churches. The collapse of centrally-planned regimes in the Soviet Union and Eastern Europe consolidated the sense of American triumphalism as the multi-polar, or even bi-polar, world gave way to a uni-polar American ascendancy. In the region, many comrades on "the left" grew weary, disillusioned and demoralised. Only those with a correct perspective of the contradictory evolution of historical forces, a realistic assessment of the possibilities and limitations of our condition, and an unswerving commitment to change, whatever the personal costs, were prepared for the dark, long days and nights of struggle ahead.

This shackling of independent, creative Caribbean thought has, of course, been met with resistance particularly in recent times consequent upon the emergence of competing poles of economic and political power internationally and the financial meltdown and economic recession, erupting in September 2008, and continuing, in the citadels of world capitalism. All of this has been occurring within the context of an all pervasive process of globalization, which contains myriad contradictions. It would have been worth hearing the insights of Gordon Lewis at this historical juncture on globalisation, its discontents, and its manifestations in the political economy of our region.

But we can perhaps gauge from his body of work, the perspective from which he would have drawn initial, not complete, sustenance to address globalisation. I feel sure that he would have turned to a young German philosopher, barely thirty years old, named Karl Marx who in the *Communist Manifesto* of 1848 wrote with much, though incomplete, prescience on globalisation:

> The Bourgeoisie cannot exist without constantly revolutionising the instruments of production, and thereby the relations of production, and with them the whole relations of society. Conservation of the old modes of production in unaltered form, was, on the contrary, the first condition of existence for all earlier industrial classes. Constant revolutionising of production, uninterrupted disturbance of all social conditions, everlasting uncertainty and agitation distinguish the bourgeois epoch from all earlier ones. All fixed frozen relations, with their train of ancient and venerable prejudices and opinions, are swept away, all new-formed ones become antiquated before they can ossify. All that is solid melts into air, all that is holy is profaned, and man is at last compelled to face, with sober senses, his real conditions of life, and his relations with his kind.

The need for a constantly expanding market for its products chases the bourgeoisie over the whole surface of the globe. It must nestle everywhere, settle everywhere, establish connections everywhere.

The bourgeoisie has through its exploitation of its world-market given a cosmopolitan character to production and consumption in every country. To the great chagrin of Reactionists, it has drawn from under the feet of industry the national ground on which it stood. All established national industries have been destroyed or are daily being destroyed. They are dislodged by new industries, whose introduction becomes a life and death question for all civilised nations, by industries that no longer work up indigenous raw material, but raw material drawn from the remotest zones, industries whose products are consumed, not only at home, but in every quarter of the globe. In place of the old local and national seclusion and self-sufficiency, we have intercourse in every direction, universal interdependence of nations. And as in material, so also in intellectual production. The intellectual creations of individual nations become common property. National one-sidedness and narrow-mindedness become more and more impossible, and from the numerous national and local literatures, there arises a world literature.

The bourgeoisie, by the rapid improvement of all instruments of production, by the immensely facilitated means of communications, draws all, even the most barbarian, nations into civilisation. The cheap prices of its commodities are the heavy artillery with which it batters down on Chinese walls, with which it forces the barbarians' intensely obstinate hatred of foreigners to capitulate. It compels all nations, on pain of extinction, to adopt the bourgeois mode of production; it compels them to introduce what it calls civilisation into their midst, i.e. to become bourgeois themselves. In one word, it creates a world after its own image.

All that and more face us in the Caribbean. Two basic options arise: Surrender and Continued Underdevelopment, on the one hand; or Creative Resistance and People's Development, on the other. This latter option is the only viable one, grounded in a people-centred vision, a philosophy of social democracy applied to our Caribbean condition, a socio-cultural rubric for the further ennoblement of our Caribbean civilisation, and a package of practical policies and programmes in the interest of our nations, region and peoples.

I have outlined in my writings in recent years the case and framework for Creative Resistance and People's Development. These offerings have covered discourses on a range of matters including: globalization; the region's political economy; job creation and wealth creation; poverty reduction; the Education Revolution; the Wellness Revolution; the fight against crime; the role of the State in the development process; the quest to build a modern post-colonial economy; the impact of the revolution in information communications technology; regional integration; the existential threat of climate change; and an independent, pragmatic, productive foreign policy. The Manifesto and other Party documents of the political party that I have the honour to lead, the Unity Labour Party of St. Vincent and the Grenadines, are replete with an array of practical, relevant policies and programmes to effect real change for the better in people's lives. After all, that is the fundamental reason for our political engagement.

Leadership of this Creative Resistance and the Quest for overall People's Development is vital. In *The Black Jacobins*, C. L. R. James had correctly observed that great leaders make history but only to the extent that history permits them. Lewis shared this view. This was, or is, not a down-grading on leadership; rather, it was/is an extolling of a requisite leadership fit for the purpose, but nevertheless constrained, and shaped, by social forces and historical circumstances. To resist creatively the ravages of a rampant globalisation while at the same time taking advantage of its positive, progressive features for people's development, demands, among other things, a leadership that not only instils in the people that which is good, but more importantly draws out of them that which is good and noble and to do so even when the people themselves do not as yet realise their goodness and nobility. This intimate, and many-layered, connection between leadership and the people in a participatory setting of good governance is at the core of driving the quest for Creative Resistance and People's Development.

To understand our Caribbean condition, and the contribution of Gordon K. Lewis to that understanding, we must necessarily turn to our history and our home-coming, a coming home to ourselves. This historical reclamation and understanding provide the basis for our future, the only time, of all time, that is ours possibly to desecrate. The avoidance of this desecration and the ensuring of our people's upliftment are at the centre of our embrace of our tomorrows with our strengths and possibilities.

The Spirit and Ideas of Maurice Bishop Are Alive in Our Caribbean Civilisation

(Feature address delivered on the occasion of the formal ceremony for the naming of the Maurice Bishop International Airport at Point Salines, Grenada, May 30, 2009.)

The spirit and ideas of Comrade Maurice Bishop, revolutionary icon and indomitable fighter for justice, popular democracy and self-determination, are alive and flourishing, among the people of Grenada and the Caribbean. This extraordinary gathering at Point Salines embraces this anti-imperialist and anti-colonialist titan whom Grenada has selflessly given to the Caribbean and the world. This belated honour of naming this international airport in his memory, and as testimonial acceptance of his heroic contribution to its construction, is just and long over-due. The vanities of parochial, vengeful and backward politics have at long last been exorcised from the citadels of the State apparatus. What we are doing today formalises a condition which has been indelibly etched in the people's collective memory for a quarter of a century. The outpouring of joy is palpable on this day which the Lord has made. Let us thus be thankful and rejoice in it.

From ancient times our people have been enjoined to honour and celebrate the lives of our fallen sons and daughters who have distinguished themselves in the service of the people. Thucydides' *History of the Peloponnesian War*, and more particularly, the "Funeral Oration" of Pericles, in extolling the glory of Greece and the majesty of its heroes, resonate with aptness for Comrade Maurice:

> For the whole earth is the sepulchre of illustrious men, nor is it the inscription on the columns in their native land alone that shows their merit, but the memorial of them, better than all inscriptions in every foreign nation, reposited more durably in universal remembrance than on their tombs. For to be lavish of life is not so noble in those whom misfortunes have reduced to misery and despair, as in men who hazard the loss of a comfortable subsistence and the enjoyment of all the blessings this world affords by an unsuccessful enterprise. Adversity, after a series of ease and affluences, sinks deeper into the heart of a man of spirit than the stroke of death insensibly received in the vigour of life and public hope.

Maurice Bishop was one such illustrious man who lived as a beacon of hope for the poor, the marginalised and the dispossessed, bore his pain and struggles with a calming equanimity. Beaten on the anvil of experience and forged in the cauldron of struggle, Maurice has emerged as the embodiment of the political virtue of our peoples' quest for self-mastery. The stone which some builders had refused has become the head cornerstone. Now that the historical dust is settling, even Maurice's severest critics and political opponents must recognise that he was one of the most outstanding sons produced by our Caribbean civilisation. Pericles had astutely commented in times of yore:

> Envy will exert itself against a competitor while life remains, but when death stops the competition, affection will applaud without restraint.

The honour being bestowed today on Maurice Bishop constitutes, too, an historical reckoning; it represents the closure of a chapter of denial. At the same time it is symbolic of a catharsis, a cleansing, which purifies and unifies with an amazing grace. Those who are blind, can now see; those who were lost, have been found.

On March 13, 1979, at 10:30 a.m., on Radio Free Grenada, Maurice Bishop, a young man barely into his 30s, Leader of the New Jewel Movement (NJM), delivered his first address to his nation as Leader of the Grenada Revolution. His opening lines were memorable, calm, sparing, and simplicity itself:

> Brothers and Sisters,
>
> This is Maurice Bishop speaking. At 4:15 a.m. this morning the People's Revolutionary Army seized control of the army barracks at True Blue.
>
> The barracks were burned to the ground. After half-an-hour struggle, the forces of Gairy's army were completely defeated, and surrendered.
>
> Every single soldier surrendered, and not a single member of the revolutionary forces was injured ….

After detailing the efforts of the People's Revolutionary Army in seizing State power, Maurice did something remarkable. He put the Revolution in the hands of the people. Thus, he intoned:

> I am appealing to all the people, gather at all central places all over the country and prepare to welcome and assist the people's armed forces when they come into your area. The revolution is expected to consolidate the position of power within the next few hours.

29

Without popular support, the Revolution would have collapsed. Fidel was later to comment that Maurice had led "a big revolution in a small country". Make no mistake about it, the Revolution and its popular acceptance provided the political foundation for the construction of the international airport at Point Salines.

Maurice addressed precisely this issue in a national broadcast on March 29, 1981, entitled "Together We Shall Build Our Airport" in the following terms:

> To begin with sisters and brothers, we must all be clear that this project represents the biggest and single most important project for our future economic development. In fact, as you all know, this represents the single biggest project ever undertaken in the history of our country. More than this, we must understand that the idea for the project has been with various Grenadian governments for 25 years or so, a reality that can be proved from the existence of numerous airport study projects dating back several years. However, with our Popular Revolution of March 13, 1979, the People's Revolutionary Government set out with seriousness and determination to transform the dream of our International Airport into a concrete reality.

Without substantial external grant assistance, in cash or kind, it was virtually impossible for the Grenada Revolution to build this international airport. From which source or sources was the grant assistance to come? The so-called traditional allies, including the United States of America, were unhelpful. Indeed, the USA, to use Maurice Bishop's own words, was in 1981 "engaged in an all out massive and vulgar attempt to dissuade various countries from attending a co-financing Conference to be hosted by the European Economic Community aimed at raising vital financing" for the International Airport Project.

At first, Maurice and his government received so little positive feedback from potential donors that he mused that the dream of its realisation would remain unfulfilled. However, solemn assurances of practical support and uplifting inspiration were to come from Fidel Castro, the leader of the Cuban Revolution, at the Non-Aligned Conference in Havana in August 1979 and again at the United Nations General Assembly gathering in October 1979. Cuba pledged immediate assistance in kind in four areas: Technical expertise, skilled manpower, heavy-duty equipment, and some construction materials such as steel and cement. In November 1979, Cuba started to make good on its commitment. The International Airport was thus on its way but much, much more was left to be done. Maurice's confidence in the Grenadian people, their Revolution, and their friends overseas, combined with determined, astute leadership, were the central pillars of turning the airport dream into reality. Maurice saw this venture as a great cause; and great causes have never been won by doubtful men and women. He and his Revolution were not doubtful!

In time, Maurice built a coalition to construct the airport. Grenada and Cuba were foundation members of that coalition. Along the way they were joined by Venezuela, Canada, Libya, and some European and Middle-Eastern countries. I was in Tripoli in July 2001, when the Libyan government forgave the residue of the indebtedness of Grenada on the airport loan in the sum of US $6 million.

Mr Chairman, the commitment of the people of Grenada to this marvel of regional and international solidarity will be told ages and ages hence. Ordinary Grenadians of all walks of life volunteered their labour, free of any remuneration, on weekends, to assist in the construction of their airport. These volunteer brigades of free labour were more than matched by the absolute determination of the Cuban workers to give life and meaning to Fidel's generosity and selflessness for which the heroic people of Cuba are known internationally. The Cuban workers toiled in comradeship with their Grenadian counterparts six days per week, twelve hours per day. Most of them volunteered to work on their rest days. One such Cuban comrade was Ramon Quintana who sadly met a sudden and unnatural death on this very site when he was crushed, accidentally, by a piece of heavy-duty equipment. We remember, especially, Ramon Quintana, today. We send special thanks to his family and to all the Cuban people. We salute Fidel; we wrap his name in glory. Fidel lives forever in the hearts and minds of Grenadians, with a love that looks on tempests and is never shaken.

We ought never to forget that those in our hemisphere who were seeking to destabilise the Grenada Revolution and to sabotage the construction of this airport were among the same persons who had, a short while before, allied themselves militarily with the racist regime of Apartheid South Africa against Nelson Mandela's African National Congress (ANC) and Augustino Neto's Movement for the Liberation of Angola (MPLA).

In that momentous struggle in Southern African, the Cubans in selfless solidarity with the freedom fighters of the ANC and MPLA, took on the mighty army of racist South Africa which was supplied by weapons from countries which sought subsequently to strangle revolutionary Grenada and its right to self-determination. The defeat, sometime later, of the hitherto impregnable army of apartheid South Africa by the Angolan and Cuban combatants at the battle of Cuito Cuanavale was instrumental in opening the prison cell of Nelson Mandela and paved the way for the founding of a free and democratic South Africa in 1991. What the Cubans did with arms in defence of the freedom of the people of Angola and South Africa, they did with construction equipment, building tools, expertise, and labour at Point Salines in Grenada. We will never forget Cuba's sacrifice, selflessness and generosity of spirit!

Let us put this phenomenal achievement of the construction of the international airport in perspective.

During the Second World War, the British and the American governments entered certain agreements concerning the leasing of large tracts of land in the British Colonial possessions in the Caribbean. In several of these countries, the Americans built international-size runways and rudimentary landside facilities to accommodate their war planes. These airports were constructed in countries with a sufficiency of flat lands to make the ventures feasible, in engineering and financial terms, in a short time. Three islands were too mountainous to benefit from this war-time American effort, namely, Dominica, Grenada and St. Vincent.

After the Second World War the Americans left the British Caribbean to the devices of the British. And the British were, as always, uninterested in enhancing the region's physical infrastructure for sustainable development. After all, the British were the colonial masters in St. Vincent and the Grenadines for some 200 years, unbroken from 1773, and they built only two small secondary schools, one for boys and one for girls, one for each century of damning colonialism. Thus, it was never contemplated that they would build or contribute to building international airports in Dominica, Grenada and St. Vincent where the terrain and topography were challenging for airport construction.

Grenada had to await the Revolution's arrival to lay the basis for the practical elaboration of the International Airport Project and its implementation. Dominica and St. Vincent and the Grenadines were insufficiently revolutionary to launch such a project. Nearly twenty-five years after the completion of the international airport at Point Salines did an anti-imperialist, nationalist and patriotic people-centred government in St. Vincent and the Grenadines, which I have the honour to head, in the evocative spirit of Maurice, commence the construction of the Argyle International Airport. It is scheduled for completion in the first quarter of 2014. As in Grenada, Cuba and Fidel have been instrumental in turning our similar dream in St. Vincent and the Grenadines into a reality. In the process we are

33

moving one mountain and three hills, filling four valleys, relocating a church and a cemetery, dismantling and causing to be built elsewhere 134 middle-income houses, and spanning a river to build our international airport. My government has fashioned a "Compact of the Willing" for this purpose, comprising the governments of Cuba, Venezuela, Trinidad and Tobago, Mexico, the Republic of China (Taiwan), Austria, Turkey, and now Iran and Libya. The Government of Dominica led by my dear friend Roosevelt Skerrit is on a similar path. We are following, in this regard, the road travelled by Maurice; a road less travelled, and that has made all the difference!

Between 1979 and 1983, imperialism told enormous lies about this airport at Point Salines and was determined to sabotage its construction. Laughable tales that the airport was for military purposes only to facilitate fighter jets and other war planes from Cuba and the Soviet Union were actually believed by supposedly serious people. Ideological blinkers and imperialist indoctrination made such people not see, or see doubles, as we say in the Caribbean. Ignorance, the mother of all suspicion, enjoyed a full flowering. A kind of "Midsummer's Night Madness" gripped the imperial ideologues; and those of a lesser light, invariably paid hacks of imperialism, voiced corresponding follies and fables about this awesome project. They must today hang their heads in shame! Do not expect apologies, only more sophistry and vaunted vanities.

One month after the triumph of the Revolution, Maurice Bishop put down his marker with crystal clarity in a national broadcast entitled "In Nobody's Backyard". It is well with our soul to quote it at some length:

> We are a small country, we are a poor country, with a population of largely African descent, we are a part of the exploited third world, and we definitely have a stake in seeking the creation of a New International Economic Order which would assist in ensuring economic justice for the oppressed

and exploited peoples of the world, and in ensuring that the resources of the land and sea are used for the benefit of all the people of the world and not for a tiny minority of profiteers. Our aim, therefore, is to join all organisations and work with all countries that will help us become more independent and more in control of our own resources. In this regard, nobody who understands present-day realities can seriously challenge our right to develop working relations with a variety of countries.

Grenada is a sovereign and independent country, although a tiny speck on the world map, and we expect all countries to strictly respect our independence just as we will respect theirs. No country has the right to tell us what to do or how to run our country, or who to be friendly with. We certainly would not attempt to tell any other country what to do. We are not in anybody's backyard, and we are definitely not for sale.

This fighting spirit, these noble ideas are what fuelled the drive to build this international airport; they, too, sustain us in our legitimate, on-going quest to further ennoble our Caribbean civilisation.

I cannot recall when I first met Maurice Bishop. It was some years prior to the Revolution, but we had known each other in revolutionary spirit long before that. So, we knew each other long before we met each other. In the decade prior to the Revolution I had come to the attention of the security forces of the region and hemisphere in the Cold War Era, not for the commission of any crime, but on account of my anti-imperialist, revolutionary democratic and socialist-oriented political activities. On October 16, 1968, at the age of 22 years, as leader of the Students' Union at the University of the West Indies, Jamaica, I led arguably the largest protest in that country since the momentous and popular anti-colonial uprising of 1938. The symbol of our defiance and affirmation of solidarity was the Guyanese scholar and revolutionary activist, Walter Rodney, who was banned by the Jamaican government from returning to his post as a university lecturer consequent upon his attendance of a Black Writers' Conference in Montreal, Canada. We were beaten and tear-gassed by the Jamaican security forces; and the leadership of the popular mass movement was vilified, harassed, and persecuted by imperialism and neo-imperial surrogates. Between October 1968 and 1979, for example, at one time or another, I was denied entry into several Caribbean countries including Grenada, St. Lucia and Antigua. In December 1979, my work permit as a university lecturer at Cave Hill was revoked by the Barbadian government and my residency in that country cancelled. I was, in the language of the day, *persona non grata* in the eyes of the established authorities. At one stroke I was denied an opportunity to work in my chosen profession in my region. I had a wife and child to feed. This is, alas, but a glimpse of those terrible days when the faces of ordinary men and women across the Caribbean were strained and anxious. Still as my Rastafarian brethren and sistren would say: "I and I survived and thrived; there is no malice, just the love of Jah from I and I."

In Grenada, Maurice Bishop and his comrades fared worst of all. They were threatened with imminent physical liquidation, a matter on which no chances could be taken, given the history of barbarism against them and the working people by the regime of the day.

I shall never forget the morning of March 13, 1979. I was living at Paradise Heights near to the university in Barbados where I was employed as a lecturer. My friend, a young St. Lucian student named Didacus Jules, who subsequently worked in the field of education under the People's Revolutionary Government and is now the Chief Executive Officer of the Caribbean Examination Council, telephoned me around 7:00 or so that morning and reported that the Gairy regime had been overthrown in Grenada, but he was unsure as to what had in fact transpired. Swiftly thereafter I ascertained the truth. I was ecstatic: Weeping had endured for a long night but joy had come that morning. God is a good God, yes He lives! A redemption song was being sung on the streets of Grenada, in the undulating valleys, on the hillsides, the plains, and beaches.

Within a week of the Revolution, Maurice invited me to visit Grenada. I did so on the second Saturday of the Revolution and immediately immersed myself in political work, under his direction, at his home where I was to be accommodated for a few days. There was so much to be done; sleep barely encroached. In any event, when I was shown my room of abode, in which was located the telecommunications equipment, I knew immediately that the nights would be long and sleepless. Frequently there were noisy radio calls for "Papa Mike", the code name for Maurice.

The next day, the second Sunday of the Revo, there was a massive rally at Sea Moon in Grenville. I rode in Maurice's vehicle with him and his wife, Angela. Along the way, people lined the streets and waved in celebration with their revered leader. At the Rally, Maurice delivered a most substantive speech, on both domestic and foreign policy matters. A significant part of his speech was in my handwriting; the other part was in his own hand. I do not know if a record of it exists anywhere.

At the onset of the French Revolution in the late 18th century, the English poet, William Wordsworth, approvingly declaimed: "Bliss was it in that dawn to be alive, but to be young was very heaven." The Revolution's enormous strength and energy flowed immensely from the work of the young people who constituted one of its important bases and from which was drawn the leadership of the principal organs of the State and Party. In retrospect, this youthfulness was also a weakness in that at critical points, a more mature, reflective, and experienced judgment would have been most helpful. Certain errors, even tragedies, could have been avoided.

Like me, most of the supporters of, and activists in, the Revolution have now lived more years than we have remaining to live. If Maurice were physically with us today, he would be sixty-five years old. He has his name on his airport before his 70th birthday, the proverbial three score and ten years. That is a cause for rejoicing.

I last saw Maurice alive in February 1983. I was passing through Grenada to get a ride on a plane going to Cuba for a celebration of the life and work of José Marti, the Cuban patriot and national hero. I spent the entire night in Maurice's company. I attended some functions with him that evening, including one at Point Salines where the Cuban engineers and construction workers were engaged in building this airport. Afterwards, we went back to the Prime Minister's residence and talked through the night, mainly about politics in the Caribbean and Grenada. I spoke to him frankly about my unease concerning certain developments in Grenada and thought that the mass support for the Revolution was becoming indifferent, in important respects. He shared my concerns and we addressed possible solutions, strategically. As comrades we were honest with each other. One day I will write about all this, God's willing.

We agreed that on my return from Cuba we would continue the conversation face-face-face. This was not to happen. The Cuban aircraft took me to Barbados; LIAT was unable to get me to Grenada that day. So, I went home to St. Vincent and the Grenadines. We kept in touch over the next few months, but I never saw my dearest Comrade and friend again. When he was murdered I cried uncontrollably like a baby. He still lives in me.

Thereafter, in the Eastern Caribbean, Rosie Douglas of Dominica, Tim Hector of Antigua, George Odlum of St. Lucia, and I, among others, kept fanning the flame for justice and freedom, for the further ennoblement of our Caribbean civilisation, and for the central struggle against imperialism. I eulogised Rosie, Tim and George at their funerals. I am the remaining survivor. I have to do their work and mine. I was never able to say of, and for, Maurice, as I did for the others, the heart-rending poetic lines of the celebrated Guyanese poet, Martin Carter, in his epic, "Death of a Comrade":

Too soon, too soon
our banner draped for you
the banner in the wind
not bound so tightly
in a scarlet fold –
not sodden
with your people's tears
but flashing on the pole
we bear aloft
down and beyond the dark lane of rags.

Dear Comrade
if it must be
you speak no more with me
nor smile no more with me
nor march no more with me
then let me take
a patience and a calm –
for even now the greener leaf explodes
sun brightens stone
and all the river burns.

Now from the mourning vanguard moving on
dear Comrade I salute you and I say
Death will not find us thinking that we die.

Maurice Bishop was a builder in the tradition of the Prophet Nehemiah. In his quest to fashion a better society for his people he was traduced by his enemies, day and night. He was a towering success; no one really remembers in glory or at all, his puny adversaries. In communion with his people and friends overseas, he set about building this international airport in a focussed manner as Nehemiah did in respect of the wall around Jerusalem which was broken and in a dilapidated condition for 112 years. Nehemiah was mocked by his enemies; they were indignant; they were moved to anger and conspiracy; they tried every ruse, including violence, to prevent the wall's reconstruction; and, when all that failed, they sought to draw him out onto the plains of Ono to ambush him. It is all reported in the book of Nehemiah. Similar things were done to, and against, Maurice. But like Nehemiah, he and his people prevailed. A committed people, properly led for noble purposes, will always triumph. Maurice's life and work taught us this splendid lesson.

Ladies and gentlemen, this ceremony would not have been possible had the people of Grenada not elected a government which pledged to do exactly what is now being done. The Grenadian people have given their overwhelming permission and approval for what is now being done in their name. In the process, an historic wrong has been righted. Today Grenada stands tall in this region and the world for this profound act of historical reclamation in which you the people view your collective achievements of the past through the prism of your own eyes and not by way of an externally-imposed imperial perspective, amidst local vanities and grudges.

Let us face it squarely, this ceremony would not have been possible without the advocacy and approval, the imprimatur, of a most humble but remarkable patriot known as Tillman Thomas, the distinguished Prime Minister of Grenada. My friend and brother, Tillman, is courageous and devoid of malice or bitterness. This easy-going but battle-hardened warrior and visionary was imprisoned by the People's Revolutionary Government headed by Comrade Maurice. I have spoken to Tillman, more than once, about his experiences in this regard. He bears no hatred for, or ill-will, to those who caused him and his family much pain and suffering. He looks forward with hope and optimism; not backwards with hurt and anguish. His Christian fortitude and love for people have touched me most deeply. His calming presence induces you to love him dearly. Grenada is blessed to have such a leader at this time. His joyous hopefulness will always endure beyond a debilitating learned hopelessness and helplessness.

The people of Grenada, in a spirit of reconciliation, have shone a light of the most illuminating clarity in the interest of their humanisation. In their actions they have accepted the poetic summation of the Caribbean poet, Daniel Williams:

> *We are all time;*
> *Yet only the future is ours*
> *To desecrate.*
> *The present is the past,*
> *And the past*
> *Our fathers' mischief.*

This naming of the Maurice Bishop International Airport is an act of the Grenadian people coming home to themselves out of their agony and compromises, their pain and joys, and their triumphs and defeats of the past. It has been an uplifting and redemptive journey. One of my favourite poets, the great Vincentian "Shake" Keane, puts it all well in his poem "Private Prayer" written in 1973 on the occasion of the publication of Walter Rodney's path-breaking volume, *How Europe Underdeveloped Africa:*

> *To understand*
> *How the whole thing run*
> *I have to ask my parents*
> *And even my daughter and son*
>
> *To understand the form*
> *Of compromise I am*
> *I must in my own voice ask*
> *How the whole thing run*

To ask
Why I don't dream
In the same language I live in
I must rise up
Among syllables of my parents
In the land which I am
And form
A whole daughter a whole son
Out of the compromise
Which I am

To understand history
I have to come home

We have come home. Grenada and Maurice have come home symbolically and in reality. I thank you and Almighty God for being present here. I feel infused by the spirit of Comrade Maurice; I believe that each of us feels it. It is a noise in our blood, an echo in our bones.

Forward Ever! Backward Never!

Errol Barrow, Our Caribbean Civilisation, and the Idea of Barbados

(The Errol Barrow Memorial Lecture delivered at the Errol Barrow Centre, University of the West Indies, Barbados, January 23, 2015.)

Introduction

January 21, 2015, was the ninety-fifth anniversary of the birth of the Right Excellent Errol Barrow, the Father of the Nation of Barbados, National Hero, and political icon of our Caribbean. On that day, and in this week, the people of Barbados and the rest of our Caribbean civilisation remember his life and work. Our collective remembrances of Errol Barrow, who died 27 years ago on June 1, 1987, occur at a time when the historical dust is settling—as it always settles—not merely to memorialise him as though entombed in a sepulchre, but to interrogate his philosophy, ideas and actions—his political praxis— in our quest to lift markedly the condition of our life, living and production. Our memory of him is in our hearts and minds, especially so in the hearts and minds of ordinary men and women whose lives he touched for the better; this collective memory, more powerful and meaningful than any engraved stone or statue, is to be transmitted enduringly to generations yet born. This annual Memorial Lecture in Errol Barrow's honour is one important conveyance by which to ensure the continuance of his ideas and spirit, and the salience of his praxis for our times and beyond. I am thus blessed to have been asked by my dear friend and Prime Minister, the Right Honourable Freundel Stuart, to deliver this Memorial Lecture. It is a signal honour and privilege for the people of St. Vincent and the Grenadines, a sister Caribbean country that Errol Barrow knew well and loved dearly.

It is generally acknowledged that Errol Barrow was not a fussy man; he did not stand on unnecessary ceremony, save in the pursuit of excellence. In accord with his intentions, no grave in the land of Barbados contains his remains. Memorably, he had addressed this very matter at the 30th Annual Conference of the Democratic Labour Party at the George Street Auditorium on August 25, 1985, in typically robust language:

> I hope that when I am called to my reckoning, since I do not require or need any outpouring of hypocrisy or glass-enclosed shrine, that they (the Press) will omit to even mention my name except to demand, if anyone tries to place me outside of the laws of Barbados, a Coroner's Inquest with full disclosure of the reasons for my withdrawal from this mortal scene. My mortal remains, after incineration, may be scattered from an aircraft in the Caribbean Sea without any of the ghoulish and undignified caterwauling that passes for services in one of our main places of public entertainment.

In one way or another, at some level or another, everyone of good sense and sensibility in our Caribbean is a disciple of Errol Barrow, even those who had tangled with him in partisan opposition, in the metaphoric jungle of competitive politics. Of course, from historical experience, we do not usually speak ill of the dead. Thucydides had drawn our attention to this general phenomenon with his insights through his survey of the *History of the Peloponnesian War*, especially the "Funeral Oration" of Pericles:

44

Envy will exert itself against a competitor when life remains, but when death stops the competition, affection will applaud without restraint.

But the admiration for Errol Barrow's extraordinary contribution to national and regional development goes way beyond the usual genuflection to a fallen hero.

So, let us together reflect on two central pillars of our present and future, through the prism of Errol Barrow's political praxis, namely the "Idea of Barbados" and its inter-connected twin, "Our Caribbean Civilisation". I begin this discourse on the latter.

Our Caribbean Civilisation

Errol Barrow always held that our Caribbean is possessed of an authentic, historically-legitimate civilisation, *sui generis*, of its own kind, with a trajectory for further ennoblement in the interest of our people's humanisation. His understanding of the concept of "Our Caribbean Civilisation" encompassed a body of civilised, and civilising, elements, including critically, a permanent presence, reflecting ownership not mere occupation, of a population in independent nationhood with global connectedness, and with a core of shared, tried and tested values, in an especial seascape and landscape, that provides a productive and technological apparatus sufficient to sustain our civilisation's socio-economic viability. A civilisation is more than a society; it is much more than a State or nation.

Errol Barrow placed his marker down unequivocally on this existential issue in a speech delivered on November 20, 1986, in the USA at the 10th Miami Conference on the Caribbean. He affirmed that:

It is dehumanising and false to view the Caribbean as potential American problems. We are peoples with an identity and a culture and a history—the Parliament of Barbados will be 350 years old in 1989. We don't need lessons in democracy from anyone. However severe the economic difficulties facing the Caribbean, we are viable, functioning societies with the intellectual and institutional resources to understand and grapple with our problems. Collectively, we have the resource potential necessary for our continued development, and, of course, we have a heritage of exquisite natural beauty entrusted to us. The Caribbean is, after all, a civilisation.

Unfortunately, many Caribbean political leaders and intellectuals, mistakenly reject the view that the Caribbean constitutes an authentic, legitimate civilisation. They tend to link, erroneously, a civilisation with an imperium as is manifested for example in the Roman, British, American, and Chinese civilisations. A civilisation does not require "empire" as a defining element. Barrow knew that the Caribbean, with no pretensions to imperium, was an island or seaboard civilisation of a special type. Through the fever of history and the process of creolisation, its population had become whole, despite some dissonance or social fracturing, out of diverse peoples—some free, most unfree—who had largely come from disparate lands, commingling and integrating with the residue of the indigenous inhabitants who had been almost totally decimated by European genocide. From culturally plural societies, in which each cultural or racial section had its own distinct pattern of socio-cultural integration, we have metamorphosed or evolved into largely homogeneous nations with a distinctive Caribbeanness which is as yet to find a single institutionalised political expression as a federal or quasi-federal entity. To be sure, our Caribbean has adopted and adapted salient features or elements from elsewhere, but we have fashioned them as our own amidst our home-grown evolutions.

A central challenge for the contemporary Caribbean is to effect a transformation from a shared Caribbeanness to a sufficiently viable, institutional expression of regional unity. This is an unfulfilled goal which Errol Barrow and his Democratic Labour Party (DLP) had set themselves at that Party's inauguration, as reflected in its foundation documents. To be sure, he placed his high-quality intellect and other resources in quest of its fulfilment but the regional political market allowed only coordinated trading arrangements in the Caribbean Free Trade Area (CARIFTA), and functional cooperation and economic integration through the Caribbean Community (CARICOM)—both of which bore the stamp of his originating architecture.

The Martinican intellectual, Edouard Glissant, in his thoughtful book, *Caribbean Discourse: Selected Essays*, addressed this very subject in a manner which would have secured Errol Barrow's approval:

> As soon as we see a political program, no matter how radical, hesitate in the face of choosing a Caribbean identity, we can offer the certain diagnosis of a hidden desire to be restrained by the limits imposed by non-history, by a more or less shameful alignment with (metropolitan) values that one can never, and with good reason, manage to control, by a fatal inability to have a sense of identity.

Errol Barrow's commitment to the idea of our Caribbean civilisation and its further ennoblement had at its centre a mature nationalism that embraced an activist regionalism and internationalism, without a descent into narrow chauvinism. His Caribbean particularism was always dialectically linked to widely-accepted universal values and humanism, without which the upliftment of any people is impossible. From the beginning, this constellation of virtues was a noise in his blood, an echo in his bones.

The affirmation of these and related principles were on display in Errol Barrow's incisive address at the Barbados Constitutional Conference in London in July 1966. It ought to be read and studied seriously, on an ongoing basis, in schools, universities and the public market place of ideas in Barbados and the Caribbean. I shall quote it at length.

Unlike many other colonial leaders, including several from the Caribbean, Errol Barrow did not go to London so much to negotiate independence as to assume it, to receive a formal constitutional imprimatur for independence that belonged to his people in fact. He did not go there to accept a Constitution drafted in the constitution-making factory of the British government's bureaucracy. His intent, and words to match, were crystal clear:

> In order that you, Mr Secretary of State, should not be incommoded by our problems, we have assumed and discharged the responsibility for producing the constitution under which the people of Barbados will continue to govern themselves after independence. As you would expect, in a country with our parliamentary traditions, this constitution was presented in draft, first to our legislature, and then to our citizens.

Barrow's assertive mood emerged from the inner strength of a finished political personality at 46 years of age; he was not a work-in-progress. Swiftly, he answered the query of "fitness for self-rule" which had pre-occupied the British, even those in a liberal tradition since the publication of John Stuart Mill's treatise, *Considerations on Representative Government*, in 1861. Errol Barrow's answer was eloquent and brimful with nationalist self-confidence:

> In our view, there can be no question whether Barbados is ripe and ready for independence. Three centuries of history answer that question in the affirmative. You have never had

to shore up our finances; you have never had to maintain or preserve public order among us.... The People of Barbados have never given you any cause to worry, and no British government has ever been forced, on our account, to vindicate its policy at the bar of international opinion.

Errol Barrow was acutely aware, as befitting one who was influenced by the philosophy and ideas of Marcus Garvey, that racism or at least racial prejudice permeated the British political psyche to the disfavour of people of African descent, in their quest for democratic self-rule. So, at the Barbados Independence Conference, he met this lurking doubt, head-on:

In assuming the burdens of independence, the people of Barbados have no illusions about their task. They are well aware that in this country, it is commonly believed, although it is not a fact, that people of African origin cannot for long maintain democratic forms of government after independence.

These people conveniently forget that the colonial system was designed not to promote free institutions but to safeguard imperial interests.

In any event, Errol Barrow asserted a Barbados exceptionalism, if one was required. He correctly declared that:

By some fortunate turn of history, the people of Barbados have managed to establish before their independence the solid framework of a free society.... They have three centuries of steady maturity to draw on and a self-confidence sprung from the management of their own affairs.

Barrow also assailed the objection of "small size", which some even in Barbados were articulating as the basis for opposing its very quest for independence. After all, Barbados was, up to then the smallest territory seeking independence from Britain, and so he was compelled to assert:

> Neither the smallness of their territory [of the people of Barbados] nor the slenderness of their physical resources deters them in the path to nationhood. They have a modest part to play in the affairs of their region, the Commonwealth and the world, and all they require from you [Secretary of State], is that you should speed them to their rendezvous with destiny sometime in 1966.

Barrow, as Premier of Barbados, had set his own time-table for the Constitutional Conference's termination and the attainment of independence for Barbados. Pointedly, infused with a profound nationalist spirit and a confidence of self, Errol Barrow accordingly directed the concluding remarks of his remarkable speech to his host, Secretary of State Fred Lee, personally:

> Mr Secretary, we have a self-imposed curfew on the duration of these discussions in that the [Barbados] government has arranged to leave the United Kingdom on the 5th of July for an equally important meeting with our partners in Canada.

> There can be no time in the circumstances for the lowing herd to wind slowly o'er the Lee.

> This, Sir, is in accord with your wishes and our intention to safeguard your person even if your office is soon to be dissolved. My Government, I assure you, Sir, will not be found loitering on colonial premises after closing time.

A Caribbean leader of rare quality had thus set his nation, Barbados, on a path, the efficacy of which even a substantial number must have doubted. Independence was a great cause; and great causes have never been won by doubtful men and women.

In our contemporary Caribbean, our leadership and people would do well to emulate Errol Barrow's mature nationalism, non-aligned posture, and profound sense of Caribbeanness. His first speech at the United Nations on the occasion of the admission of Barbados to membership of that august body in December 1966, is memorable for its oft-repeated tag-line "Friends of all, satellites of none". But in that address he articulated themes which remain supremely relevant today, including: The pursuit of foreign policy as an extension, not a contradiction of domestic policy; the necessity and desirability of upholding the vital role of small states at the United Nations based on the doctrine of "the equality of states"; the obligation to battle for the elimination of global poverty as a prerequisite to the maintenance of international peace and justice; the importance of multi-lateralism, not super-power triumphalism in world affairs; and the requirement of large and small nations to respect, and abide by, the fundamental principles and ideals, of the Charter of the United Nations.

The strength and assertiveness of Barrow's independent outlook and Caribbeanness are likely to startle timid souls today who have allowed their thought processes to be enslaved to the Washington Consensus and a modern imperium which parades under the ideological label of "neo-liberalism". Take for example Barrow's blast against President Ronald Reagan's shameless appropriation of an independent, regionally-inspired unifying concept of "the Caribbean Basin"—the Caribbean the Latin American countries washed by the Caribbean Sea—and the bastardisation of it into an American Trojan-horse called the Caribbean Basin Initiative (CBI) which had its central focus reserved for a non-Caribbean country, El Salvador.

In a News Conference in Barbados, dated April 22, 1982, on the CBI, Errol Barrow traced the origin and elaboration of the concept of the "Caribbean Basin" to Prime Minister Eric Williams of Trinidad and Tobago and the regional titan, Williams Demas. Under that rubric fell home-grown Caribbean initiatives such a the Caribbean Food Plan; the Trinidad-Jamaica-Guyana-Suriname and Mexico agreement for joint practical action in the bauxite/aluminium and petroleum industries; and Venezuela's proposal to the Caribbean on the sale of fuel on concessionary credit terms, which in many ways resemble the updated, and current, Petro Caribe arrangements devised through the leadership of Presidents Hugo Chavez and Nicolas Maduro.

At this News Conference in April 1982, Errol Barrow stated, thus:

> What I wish to reiterate, for the last time, is that none of these Plans called for any outside expertise, or any outside financial assistance. As a matter of fact, the main rationale of the plan was to make us independent of refineries of aluminium outside, make us independent of external shipping, and make us independent of the imports of food from countries which were outside the Caribbean.

Over the last twenty years, few—hardly any—Caribbean leaders or Caribbean intellectuals have written or spoken in such visionary terms; and hardly any debate in public fora has addressed, in any focussed way, any of these questions or variants thereof.

On the contrary, currently, when independent Caribbean or Caribbean–Latin American spaces are elaborated for action to advance our people's interest, negativism and learned helplessness, by those who look forward to the past, are held aloft by several Caribbean academics and media practitioners as the preferred responses or options. Take the case of the proposal for Venezuela's sale of "fuel for the Caribbean", on concessionary terms, in Barrow's time and currently under Petro Caribe.

Let us listen carefully to Barrow's words at his April 1982 News Conference:

> Now, where did the Venezuela come in on this? The Venezuelans, 'round about 1974, made an offer that they would sell [crude] oil to the territories at a price of $6.00 per barrel.

> ...The Venezuelans, being members of OPEC (Organisation of Petroleum Exporting Countries), could not break that agreement; so what the Venezuelans said they would do was to give us credit; in other words we would pay them $6.00 a barrel and, let us say the price was $12.00 per barrel just for the sake of argument, they would sell us at $6.00 a barrel and the other $6.00 we could use locally for economic development, and it would be a book entry which we would owe the Venezuelan government—theoretically we would owe the Venezuelans this money, but I doubt that the Venezuelan government would ever want to collect that money. There again an initiative coming from within the Caribbean.

> You will ask me now, what happened to the plan. It is a very sad story.

> Some Foreign Ministers got together in New York.... These Foreign Ministers, having heard about the plan from some of their leaders like Forbes Burnham of Guyana, Dr Eric Williams, myself, and the President of Venezuela, decided that they would summon their own meeting and invited 'Marish and Parish', 'Sam Cow and Duppy', everybody. All the OAS (Organisation of American States) people—everybody, because they wanted to get international limelight.

They held the meeting at the time of the United Nations General Assembly in New York, without authority whatsoever from Dr Williams, the President of Venezuela, or anybody else. At that meeting, they spoke about the Caribbean Basin Plan, without anybody telling them to do so. They called the American press, and decided that they were going to have the first meeting in Caracas, Venezuela.

...They meant well, but they wanted to get a little limelight, a little credit.

The upshot of all this was that suspicions were sown; the process was manipulated externally. The meeting never took place whether in Caracas, Port-of-Spain, or Bridgetown.

The similarities between the Venezuela proposal and the current Petro Caribe arrangements are self-evident. The unacceptable derision and facile opposition to Petro Caribe from some quarters, under promptings from external agencies, can never persuade the government of St. Vincent and the Grenadines to unsign or terminate Petro Caribe which has proven to be quite beneficial to the people of St. Vincent and the Grenadines. It is for us a centre-piece of ALBA, of which every independent member-state of the Organisation of Eastern Caribbean States (OECS) is now a full member; it is, too, an important corner stone of the Community of States of Latin America and the Caribbean (CELAC) , a regional grouping which includes all the independent countries of the Caribbean, including Cuba and Our America, but excluding our traditional and enduring allies, USA and Canada, with which we are linked in the hemispheric OAS, which sadly excludes Cuba.

I have absolutely no doubt that these crafted instruments of Petro Caribe and CELAC would have met with Errol Barrow's approval. It would forever be recalled that, a mere six years after Barbados became an independent nation, on December 8, 1972, Barrow joined the democratically-elected leaders of Guyana, Jamaica and Trinidad in having their respective governments establish formal diplomatic relations with Cuba, in the teeth of opposition from, and unacceptable machinations by, the government of the USA. President Barack Obama and President Raul Castro of Cuba, are today seeking to mend the hemispheric fracture which for too long has been fuelled by anachronistic Cold War thinking, presidential politics of Southern Florida, and vanities and vainglories associated with hegemonic power.

The well-grounded, and finished, personality known as Errol Walton Barrow in his world outlook, practical life and living, and his political actions in our Caribbean civilisation reflected the insights of the Mexican Nobel Laureate for Literature, Octavio Paz, in his book *The Labyrinth of Solitude and Other Writings*:

> Civilisation is a society's style, its way of living and dying. It embraces the erotic and culinary arts, dancing and burial; courtesies and curses; work and leisure; rituals and festivals; punishments and rewards; dealings with the dead and with ghosts who people our dreams; attributes towards women and children, old people and strangers, enemies and allies; eternity and the present; the here and now and the beyond. A civilisation is not only a system of values but a world of forms and codes of behaviour, rules and exceptions. It is society's visible side—institutions, monuments, work, things—but it is especially its submerged, invisible side, beliefs, desires, fears, repressions, dreams.

The geographic location of the Caribbean close to the wealthiest and most powerful country in world history, the United States of America, has had an immense impact on our region and its people. Our geography has been as important in the shaping of our civilisation as our history and our demographics. Had we been located near to Vladivostok or in the Taiwan straits, other overweening presences would have preoccupied us.

Inevitably, for us today, as indeed it was for Errol Barrow, we must come to terms with our hegemonic neighbour to the north. All Latin America and the Caribbean have to fashion an efficacious many-sided relationship between our island civilisation and the continental civilisation of the United States of America. The USA has a population of over 300 million; CARICOM, excluding the 10 million in Haiti, has a population of some 6 million; Barbados has a population of 270,000; St. Vincent and the Grenadines, 110,000. Mexico, with a population of 110 million, has this challenge, and opportunity, too, in crafting its relationship with the USA.

Octavio Paz, with his towering intellect and native sensibility, addressed comparatively the civilisations of Mexico and the USA, with lessons for our Caribbean, thus:

> Of course, the differences between Mexico and the United States are not imaginary projections but objective realities. Some are quantitative, and can be explained by the social, economic, and historical development of the two countries. The more permanent ones, though also a result of history, are not easily definable or measurable. I have pointed out that they belong to the realm of civilisation, that fluid zone of imprecise contours in which are fused and confused ideas and beliefs, institutions and technologies, styles and morals, fashions and churches, the material culture and the evasive reality which we rather inaccurately call 'the genie des peuples'. The reality to which we give the name civilisation does not allow of easy definition. It is each society's vision of the world and also its feeling about time; there are nations hurrying toward the future, and others whose eyes are fixed on the past.

For Errol Barrow, one central question in our Caribbean civilisation was, and still is: "What kind of image do we have of ourselves?" In an address to a political rally in Bridgetown on May 13, 1986, at which the DLP's 27 candidates for the general elections of May 28, 1986, were introduced, Errol Barrow spoke with profundity in clear language on this matter:

> I wish to speak to you...this evening about you. About yourself. I want to know what kind of mirror image do you have of yourself? That is what I am concerned about.... Do you really like yourselves? Because you can never really like anybody unless you first like yourself. There are too many people in Barbados who despise themselves and their dislike of themselves reflects itself in their dislike of other people—people who live next door to them, members of their family, husbands and wives, and the ox and the ass and the stranger within the gates.

> ...Let me tell you what kind of mirror image I have of you, or what the Democratic Labour Party has of you. The Democratic Labour Party has an image that the people of Barbados would be able to run their own affairs, to pay for the cost of running their own country, to have an education system which is as good as what can be obtained in any industrialised country, anywhere in the world.

> ...What kind of image do you have of yourself when you allow the mothers of this nation to be beasts of burden in the sugar-cane fields?

> ...What kind of mirror image do the people of the Barbados Workers' Union—have even of you or themselves?

...Why should only one man have a mirror image of you that you do not want to have of yourself? What kind of society are we striving for? There is no point in striving for Utopia, but you do not realise your potential.

...There is another small country which is run by a friend of mine. The country has 210 square miles; it is 40 square miles bigger than Barbados.... It is Singapore of Lee Kuan Yew. Barbados has 250,000 people; Singapore has two and a half million on an island just a little larger than Barbados.

They don't have any sugar plantations; they don't have enough land to plant more than a few orchids on. It is one of the orchid centres of the world.... They don't have enough land to plant a breadfruit tree in the backyard.

...They have developed an education system but they are teaching people things that are relevant to the 21st century. They are not teaching people how to weed by the road. They are in the advance of the information age.

But you know the difference between you and them. They have got a mirror image of themselves.... They have self-respect. They have a desire to move their country forward by their own devices. They are not waiting for anybody to come and give them handouts.

Repeatedly Errol Barrow emphasised that though the Barbadian or Caribbean person is not better than anyone else, no one is better than us; different, but not better. This is the centre that holds together the idea and reality of our Caribbean civilisation, which alone represents the socio-cultural defence, nay, inoculation, against a marauding cultural imperialism, parading as universal but fundamentally in service of a globalised imperium.

No progressive society or civilisation has ever been built on leisure, pleasure or nice-time. It has to be constructed on a base of hard and smart, productive labour. Laziness is an absence of virtue. To be sure, leisure and pleasure are necessary and desirable in life but it has to be paid for through productive endeavours. Errol Barrow believed all this and articulated these views publicly. Accordingly, he sought, with commendable success, to diversify the plantation economy into tourism, light manufacturing, and an array of services, including finance, banking and insurance, so as to create wealth and jobs for the people as a whole. The central hand-maidens in this diversification process were a quality educational system, a modern health-delivery system, marked enhancements in the physical infrastructure, reforms in the state administration, good governance arrangements, deepening regional integration, and a pragmatic and principled foreign policy.

These policies and programmatic achievements under Errol Barrow's leadership were not merely an exercise in political modernisation, as some critics aver. They were an incredible acceleration of a social democratic revolution which commenced in the anti-colonial uprising of 1937, and is yet fully to run its course. These measures constituted, in their aggregation, a further ennoblement and advance of our Caribbean civilisation. In the process, the "Idea of Barbados" emerged as an especial contribution to our Caribbean.

The Idea of Barbados

In February 2014, I authored a brief paper entitled "The Idea of Barbados". It found its way into the public fora by way of the internet. As someone who is not exactly a "stranger in the gates" of Barbados, though not holding that country's citizenship, I considered it opportune to contribute to the public discourse on the way forward for Barbados and our Caribbean civilisation. There has been so much negativism and learned helplessness about our region's and Barbados' travails that I thought that demagoguery and our Caribbean tendency of "beating up on ourselves" were in danger of triumphing in a situation which demanded critical, independent thought. The philosophy and achievements of Errol Barrow were the starting point which prompted me in the direction of fleshing out "the Idea of Barbados".

Barbados is an idea which has, over time, become manifest in reality. The idea of Barbados encompasses more than a nation-state or a national community. To be sure, it flows from a national community which has been in ownership, not residence, of an especial or particular landscape and seascape. Still, it is more than this; and it assumes a veritable autonomy as a category beyond the community. The Barbadian diaspora, scattered overseas, has come to draw from this "specialness" known as the idea of Barbados. This idea acknowledges that Barbados is unique, *sui generis*, of its own kind. It is connected to, nay derived from, the physical and historical condition of Barbados, yet transcends it.

The unique "idea of Barbados" does not, and cannot, make Barbados immune from the universal "laws" of history, society or political economy. Indeed, the idea of Barbados has been fashioned through a parallelogram of historical forces and contemporary circumstances, global and regional, which have shaped and conditioned the home-grown evolutions, adaptations, alterations, and changes.

More than any other Caribbean society with the possible exception of Cuba, Barbados has arrived at a place where its uniqueness represents a model of governance, political economy, way of life, and social order that invites emulation elsewhere in the Caribbean and further afield, albeit with appropriate amendments. Barbados' high quality governance and level of human development have been a marvel to objective observers, including reputable international agencies. On a wide range of governance and developmental indices, Barbados is in the top rank globally; indeed, overall, it is a developing country with developed nations' governance and human development attainments. All this is extraordinary for a country of 166 square miles and a quarter million people, which is less than 200 years removed from slavery and less than 50 years as an independent nation!

I make bold to say that other CARICOM member-states aspire to being an "idea" but none has quite achieved that status, even though each possesses its particular nationalism. In this comparative sense, Jamaica is a brand but not an idea. Rastafarianism, Bob Marley, Usain Bolt and Sandals have helped to shape the Jamaican brand, a marketing tool to attract visitors, but it is not a transcendental idea which infuses the body politic and society. Trinidad is an incomplete national formation engulfed by rising lawlessness and propped up by oil; the Trinidadian intellectual, Kirk Meighoo, calls his country "a half-made society" in his book so entitled, and published in 2003. Guyana's natural condition is still largely untamed; a nation that possesses enormous potential, but yet not close to being realised. The member-states of the OECS in one way or another, consciously or unconsciously, aspire to the Barbados "model". "Successful" British colonies such as Bermuda and the British Virgin Islands possess an artificiality that overwhelms their indigenous vitality. The French overseas territories of Martinique and Guadeloupe are subsidised enclaves in the region, in search of a Caribbean identity. Puerto Rico is a Caribbean outpost of the American empire, a confused and inchoate territory with an ill-defined future.

This idea of Barbados is not coterminous with a narrow chauvinism, island nationalism or a jaundiced arrogance, though some within and without Barbados may mistake or confuse these with the uplifting "idea" itself. The "idea of Barbados" has saved Barbados in the past and will surely enable Barbados to meet successfully its current economic challenges brought on largely, though not exclusively, by the prolonged global economic slow-down from 2008, and continuing.

Barbados is at once the most conservative and the most progressive society in the Caribbean, bar none! It extols continuity yet engineers, and embraces, change. It is the only Caribbean country that has had, since conquest and settlement, unbroken representative government albeit on a restrictive franchise until universal adult suffrage in 1944. It is the first Caribbean country to have attained mass adult literacy, universal primary and secondary education, and "free" university education. It is the first Caribbean country to have transformed its economy from sugar to tourism, international financial services, and other services. Very early it embraced the Caribbean Court of Justice and cut the judicial umbilical cord with the British Privy Council, yet it values its connection with the British Crown. Barbados is "rigid with starch and Anglicanism", to use Gordon Lewis' telling phrase of 1968, but is more relaxed, informally, about homosexuality than any other Caribbean society. It places a premium on the maintenance of law and order, yet zealously guards individual rights and freedoms. And the list goes on!

Errol Barrow has been in the forefront of crafting the transformation which has given rise to this "Idea of Barbados".

In Barbados, there is an invisible "genius of the people" which is the foundation of the idea of Barbados. Modern social scientists refer to this social foundation as "social capital" but it is more than this. I find the category of "social capital" an inadequate proxy for the grounded common sense of Barbadians, their social solidarity, their ability to enhance their capacity to come to terms with their condition and environment, and to address in an efficacious way any bundle of challenges that arise. Other Caribbean societies, including St. Vincent and the Grenadines, display these qualities, but Barbados seems to have them to an extraordinary degree.

There is an undoubted Barbadian sensibility which informs or shapes the individual and collective responses of the Barbadian people. Many other Caribbean nationals perceive this, quite wrongly, as a sense of "Bajan superiority". It is not that; it is an attribute of quiet assurance, a manifestation of the virtue of self-mastery. That is the well-spring of a civil, and civilised, people steeped in progressive values, but on the bedrock of a bundle of core values lodged in the social consciousness. More than perhaps any other Caribbean nationals, they, following the teachings and example of Errol Barrow, appreciate that a progressive society is not built on leisure, pleasure and nice-time, but on hard, smart, productive effort. All this is part of the idea of Barbados. Still, this productive base is unlikely to realise its full potential without its enlargement in a CARICOM Single Market and Economy. Barrow realised that too!

An acute and dispassionate observer of Barbados notices a distinctiveness that goes beyond, and is partly evident from, an especially unique accent in speech; a restraint in the use of bombast in day-to-day language; an intolerance of slip-shod work; an insistence that government delivers basic services of quality; a settled, though uneven, "mirror image" of themselves; and an elemental patriotism devoid of gaudy exhibitionism. These observances are evident in the outlook of Barbadians of all walks of life: Rank-and-file Bajans, intellectuals, business folks, Bajan Rastafarians, writers/performers in the field of the creative imagination, civil society leaders, and assorted professionals.

However, cultural imperialism is in grave danger of undermining these Barbadian values and elevating a coarseness in hitherto civilised discourse. Further, the plantation legacies touching and concerning race, intertwined with class, have yet to be fully exorcised from the economy, society and polity. Oft-times, cultural imperialism buttresses these legacies of subordination and super-ordination.

I have observed that, generally-speaking, the best and brightest of Barbados enter its public service, whether in the civil service, the teaching service, the judiciary, or politics. At the leadership levels it has been blessed by brilliant and grounded personalities such as Grantley Adams, Errol Barrow, Tom Adams, Bernard St. John, Henry Forde, Ritchie Haynes, Erskine Sandiford, Owen Arthur, David Thompson, Freundel Stuart, and Mia Mottley. Surely, this constellation constitutes an abundance of riches over a sixty year period. Of this galaxy, I am of the considered opinion that Errol Barrow is the greatest leader that our CARICOM region has thrown up since universal adult suffrage. In national and regional impact and influence, Barrow compares with Lee Kuan Yew of Singapore. This high quality leadership over a sustained period is a manifestation, and a buttress, of the idea of Barbados. In the complex and competitive modern global circumstances, the nurturing of continued quality leadership is an awesome challenge for Barbados. The idea of Barbados is in danger of being undermined if the political system fails to renew and replenish, on an on-going basis, its leadership stock from the best and brightest of Barbados.

I am satisfied that the "idea of Barbados" is the vehicle through which Barbados will successfully meet its current and prospective economic challenges. The idea of Barbados is a shared experience of Barbadians; it belongs to them. However, this shared experience must become a conscious expression and a fully-articulated language for action. It is the frame of reference for continuity and change, orderly governance and profound alterations in the political economy to accommodate the circumstances at hand.

In this vein, I pose an overarching query which I raised a year ago in the context of my 2014 Budget Address for St. Vincent and the Grenadines. The query for Barbados is this: Can the socio-economic model initiated by Errol Barrow, perfected by subsequent governments, and which came to maturation under Owen Arthur, be sustained in a period of prolonged global economic slow-down and continued economic uncertainty? If the answer is "Yes", a temporising wait-and-see attitude or approach may be in order. If the answer is "No", alterations and adaptations appropriate to the condition are clearly necessary and desirable.

In St. Vincent and the Grenadines, and I suspect in Barbados, a temporising or wait-and-see is out of the question.

An appropriate strategic framework, balancing prudence and enterprise, coupled with specially-targeted interventions, is likely to foster economic growth and fiscal consolidation.

The correct answer to the overarching query which I have posed, within the articulated context of "the idea of Barbados", is likely to yield uplifting results. Thus, rather than propose a particular policy without an articulated context, the policy should be put within the appropriate strategic framework. Once it is appreciated that the extant socio-economic model is not sustainable at a time of a prolonged global economic slow-down and that Barbados has always triumphed in challenging circumstances, the people are likely to respond understandingly and favourably. So, for example, a contribution from students to their own educational investment at the tertiary level is less likely to be opposed if the altered circumstances are understood and properly explained. If the answer to the overarching query, articulated context and strategic framework (including targeted interventions) are fully elaborated, references to "Barrow's legacy" or "Bajan's birthright" would be seen as mechanistic and thus intellectually/practically untenable. The foundation-stone of Errol Barrow's ideas and political praxis must be appropriately interrogated and the underlying principles and practices applied, not in rote fashion, but in their essence, and with flexibility as the practical circumstances admit.

I am grappling with similar considerations and policy/ programmatic issues in St. Vincent and the Grenadines. Unless we have intellectual clarity ourselves we are likely to lose our way.

The issues at stake for St. Vincent and the Grenadines, and probably for Barbados, include: Efficient public expenditure; the containment of recurrent expenditure; efficacious debt management; optimal tax administration; economic growth within the context of an optimal-functioning CSME; job and wealth creation; social cohesion and a reduction in social inequality. These are very challenging and not amenable to quick fixes, particularly in small, open, resource-challenged economies in the context of a global economic slow-down. Some of the chatterati, with their feet firmly planted in the air, have all the facile answers, but no responsibility for their invariable wrong-headedness.

Fundamentally, "the idea of Barbados" faces enormous challenges from the process of globalisation and its attendant discontents. Globalisation facilitates an increasing homogenisation of culture propagated by a dominant cultural imperialism. Globalisation is impatient of "localization", but the idea of Barbados strengthens the quest for a particular space within a wider universalism. This dialectical engagement between "the local" and "the global" does not necessarily presage an undermining of the idea of Barbados, but an enrichment of it. Still, it is a challenging endeavour. We must have faith that the idea of Barbados will endure, but faith is made complete or perfect with deeds.

Errol Barrow's Transformative Leadership

In assessing the influence, quality and transformative leadership of Errol Barrow, we ought to resist the temptation of focussing on the multitude of individual and tactical decisions which any political leader, and particularly those in our small, Caribbean countries, may make. Instead, our emphasis ought to be on the strategic approaches elaborated, adopted and implemented. Any political leader who is required to make numerous particularistic decisions, as Caribbean Prime Ministers do on a daily basis, relating to this or that matter, is likely to chalk up some errors relating to persons and things. Undoubtedly, an individual here or there may have a

Prime Ministerial discretion exercised unfavourable to him or her but which in no way undermines, hampers, or reflects adversely on the forward thrust of the society. Leaders are invariably assessed on the larger strategic issues, even though it is of importance always to get the small things right. Of course, if negligence and wrong-headedness on the small things are so egregious and widespread, the haunting spectre of maladministration may become so pervasive that it subverts strategic accomplishments. This was not evident in Barrow's case. In all assessments, the context and circumstances are of fundamental account.

In a speech delivered in 1980 at a graduation ceremony of the University of the West Indies, Cave Hill, Barbados, one of the foremost writers of the creative imagination in the 20th century, George Lamming, had this to say:

> Men make their own history but we can only make that portion of it which our concrete circumstances allow. We do not choose the time or place of our birth, nor the parents who make this possible; but the process of our thought, the hidden nature of our needs, the character and quality of our imagination may be decisively influenced by these origins. Our struggle towards freedom is experienced always within the external constraints of nature and the invincible limitations of our own consciousness.

Indeed, this is Lammings' refinement of Karl Marx's brilliant work entitled *The Eighteenth Brumaire of Louis Napoleon*, published in 1869, and C. L. R. James' further contribution on this subject in his path-breaking volume, *The Black Jacobins*, the authoritative text on Toussaint L'Ouverture and the Haitian Revolution.

I am sure that the insights of Lamming, James and Marx are helpful in the assessment of Errol Barrow's leadership and his immense contributions, amidst his much lesser failures or limitations. Such an assessment must always avoid abstractions and stylised polemics.

Although this is not an occasion for an exploration of Errol Barrow's biography, we acknowledge the influences on, and the shaping of, his political praxis as leader: His parenting and family; his socialisation generally; his education and training; his active service in the Second World War; the shaping of his nationalism, regionalism, and social democracy in London as a student; his experiences as a lawyer in Barbados; his profound grasp of the nature of our Caribbean's physical environment (land, sea, air) and its impact on our people; his political activism from the early 1950s; the history of British colonialism struggles world-wide; the advances made by social democracy and socialism globally; the contradictions and evolution of the plantation economy in Barbados; the nature of the dominant bourgeois political economy globally and the internationalisation of monopoly capital.

Barrow's achievement in leading the transformation of Barbados from a veritable plantation "village" into a modern, sophisticated nation is now legendary. But his is not mere legend; it is factual. Brilliant as the political scientist, Gordon Lewis, was in his magisterial volume *The Growth of the Modern West Indies*, published in 1968, he was in error in his assessment of Errol Barrow as simply "a moderniser". To be fair to Lewis, he had not yet seen the full flowering of Barrow's social democracy, applied to the domestic and external circumstances of Barbados. My settled view of the whole of Barrow's record is that he was a transformative and not a transactional leader. "Tom" Adams was of the latter type.

Errol Barrow's "social democracy", which he sometimes labelled as "socialism", was creative in its application in a small social economy with exchange relations with international capitalism, ravaged by the incubus of colonialism—long after colonialism had departed—

and the legacies of the plantation system, in a world dismissive, and ignorant of, or even hostile to, the condition of small states. To describe him, and his political praxis, as "Fabian socialist" and mere "moderniser" is to stylise the facts in search of a theory of explanation. In his life's work, particularly as Premier and later as a long-serving Prime Minister of Barbados, he contributed in an extraordinary, and heroic, way to the creation of an equality of opportunities, an education revolution, a far more equal society, a safe and secure country, a massive improvement in living standards, enhanced good governance, independent nationhood, modernisation grounded in a tried and tested core of values of our Caribbean civilisation, and an enhanced image of self.

Barrow's leadership was of an especial high quality. To be sure, he inspired the people whom he led; but more importantly he drew out of them what was good and noble in them; oft-times he drew out goodness and nobility which the people did not as yet know that they possessed. So, he did not simply instill; he did something more profoundly lasting; and he caused his people to deliver above the very limitations which they had imposed on themselves. Barrow assessed adroitly his people's possibilities and limitations, strengths and weaknesses, and drew out of them far more than what they knew that they possessed. Frankly, this is revolutionary leadership in societies accustomed to "commandist" modes of leadership, propped up by gubernatorial and colonial inheritances. And he did it all without posturing, without pandering to backwardness, without a facile genuflection to passing fads, or the naked opportunism of rootless persons who believe in little or nothing save and except the pursuit of an insatiable thirst for a demeaning, and illusory, power.

Errol Barrow's towering accomplishments were not accompanied by any sacralisation of personal power. His mystique arose not from any "sacredness", contrived or otherwise, but from humility, commitment to the people, and a simple lifestyle. He eschewed, nay, opposed, the "Presidential" demeanour and imitative style, initiative mockeries so evident in post-colonial leaderships in our region and elsewhere. He turned askance against official corruption, railed against it, and succeeded in keeping it at a minimal level. He undoubtedly would have concurred with H. A. Vaughn's scornful portrayal of "Certain Demagogues":

> *Like blackbirds in their shiny coats*
> *Pricking and lifting spry, proud feet,*
> *Bickering and picking sodden oats*
> *From horses' offal in the street.*

Today in our Caribbean, the political gospel of hopelessness and helplessness by so many who occupy high perches in politics, academia, the church, business, and the commentariat, would have found no support from Errol Barrow. He was always positive about the possibilities, abilities and resources of our Caribbean to sustain and advance our civilisation. He worried not about adversities and limitations; rather, he framed them into his personal or political calculus in moving forward. He never forgot our blessings, our strengths and possibilities, which are huge. One senses that his early socialisation and his life experiences had imbued him with the age-old lesson from the Sermon on the Mount as told in the *Book of Matthew*:

> O you of little faith? So do not worry, saying, 'What shall we eat?' or 'What shall we drink?' or 'What shall we wear?' For the pagans run after all these things, and your heavenly Father knows that you need them....Therefore, do not worry about tomorrow, for tomorrow will worry about itself. Each day has enough trouble of its own.

This settled, positive outlook is needed now more than ever in our public discourses. To be sure, in each of us there is a tension between "the positive" and "the negative". Which will triumph? The one which we feed! The feeding of "the positive" and not "the negative" is vital for individual and collective advancement, indeed, redemption.

The strand of overwhelming negativism and undue worry engendered by those who ought to know better, and accepted uncritically by those who know not, is frequently conjoined with an undue haste to get things done, which bears no relationship to the real world or the actual, concrete conditions of life and living. In St. Vincent and the Grenadines, the folk have a profound saying: "Hurry, hurry bird nah build good nest."

Elias Canetti, the distinguished European Nobel Laureate for Literature drew our attention to one dimension of this "avoidance of the concrete" in his remarkable book entitled *The Conscience of Words and Earwitness* published in 1987:

> Among the most sinister phenomena in intellectual history is the avoidance of the concrete. People have had a conscious tendency to go first after the most remote things, ignoring everything they stumble over close by. The élan of outgoing gestures, the boldness and adventure of expeditions to faraway places camouflage their motives. The not infrequent goal is to avoid what lies near because we are not up to it.... One would have to be very narrow-minded to condemn this adventurousness of the mind even though it sometimes comes from obvious weaknesses. It has led to an expansion of our horizon, of which we are proud. But the situation of mankind, today, as we all know it, is so serious that we have to turn to what is closest and most concrete.

The observation, thus, of the concrete condition at hand is the starting point of scientific enquiry from which hypotheses emerge for testing on the way to a determination of the causal relationships or interconnections, amidst all their contradictions, within the real condition. It is from this process of intellectual probing, which includes the drawing upon the storehouse of accumulated thought and wisdom, and study of the data, that theories of explanation are arrived at, and fine-tuned, for public policy and programmes in the people's interest. This fact-based enquiry and analysis, policy-making, and programmatic implementation are at odds with the wild abstractions, invariably fuelled by hidden motives or agendas, designed to hold aloft that which is strategically negative and subversive of the public good.

The intellectual haste, which prompts negative abstractions, is propelled by persistent demands for "instant" delivery of this or that. So, instant coffee, instant cocoa, instant communication, and so forth, fashion unwittingly, a mentality for instant satisfaction of public goods and services, without regard for the means or resources sufficient for that satisfaction, instantly or at all.

Upon a close examination of Errol Barrow's political praxis, one discerns these multiple considerations. At the core is an acknowledgement that public responsibility of leaders has to be matched by citizenry or individual, responsibility in every sphere of life and living. Bickering constantly about others' efforts without a delivery of your own optimal output to add value to the enterprise, achieves one thing only: a boosting of the complaining industry. And those who hunger always for power, glory and material well-being are likely to find that their longing is insatiable, in the real world; sadly, their desire almost always outruns their capacity or opportunity for attainment; thus, perpetual dissatisfaction becomes their lot, resulting in unnecessary and oft-times dangerous conflicts and divisiveness. No public policy can quell this permanent state of dissatisfaction driven by such personal, insatiable hunger.

Errol Barrow taught us all this. The study of his praxis remains indispensable for the further advancement of our Caribbean civilisation, and the Idea of Barbados.

Nationalism, Regionalism and Internationalism in the Political Praxis of Cheddi Jagan of Guyana

(Address delivered as the Cheddi Jagan Annual Lecture 2015, Monday, April 13, 2015, at Georgetown, Guyana, sponsored by the Cheddi Jagan Centre.)

Preface

At the outset, let me issue a disclaimer: I am not here to support any political party in the impending general elections. Indeed, even if I were inclined to offer such support, it would be entirely futile since I have no influence whatsoever on the electorate of Guyana. Further, I have good friends in the several political combinations contending for political office and I thus have no desire either to embarrass or disappoint any of them.

I should point out that this lecture was scheduled to be delivered one month ago, but it was postponed, at my request, to facilitate my availability.

I am here this evening to make a contribution to the on-going conversation about the nationalism, regionalism, and internationalism of one of Guyana's iconic political leaders, Dr Cheddi Jagan, who was also one of my dear friends, comrades, and mentors.

Introduction

Cheddi Jagan's life experiences undoubtedly fashioned his vision, philosophy, socio-cultural outlook, political programmes and policies. His remarkable intellect and selfless persona shaped his predispositions and ideas. It can be said, as was said of the prophets Isaiah and Jeremiah, and the Apostle Paul, that he was set apart from his mother's womb to be what he became.

Cheddi Jagan, child of indentured servants from India, was born in rural, colonial British Guiana on March 22, 1918, a few months after the Bolsheviks stormed to power in the Soviet Union and just a few months before the winding down of the tumultuous First World War. He died on March 6, 1997, shortly before his 79th birthday, as the serving President of the Republic of Guyana. By then the Soviet Union had disintegrated after some seventy years of over-rule by a Communist Party, which along the way had strayed from several of the theoretical precepts of its foundation gospel, Marxism – Leninism. By then, too, the People's Republic of China had evolved from the condition of a poor, underdeveloped country to become a global economic power-house, having ditched Mao Tse Tung's "great leap forward" of socialism in China for a modernising capitalism under the political leadership of a Communist Party. At Cheddi Jagan's death, too, a rampant imperialism under the guise of modern globalisation was in the process of consolidation, led by monopoly capital in the United States of America, Europe, and the so-called "emerging markets" in hitherto underdeveloped countries on the periphery of imperial hegemony. A confident, and even boastful, global capitalism enwrapped in the liberal democratic garb of the Washington Consensus declared itself triumphant and even proclaimed, in the words of one of its transient high priests that "the end of history", the world's ideal, had arrived.

Meanwhile, millions globally were still starving; global diseases, communicable and non-communicable, were spreading at an alarming rate; mother earth was being despoiled as man-made climate change caused the alteration of weather patterns and threatened humanity's existential condition; and multiple wars raged across the world amidst heightening political instability globally.

In 1918 when Cheddi Jagan was born, there was hardly a radio in his rural village and not many in capital city, Georgetown. There were few motor vehicles in Guyana, and technological development was at a low level. When he died in 1997, mobile phones were becoming widely available and within a few years after his death they were everywhere in the hands of everyone. The streets of Georgetown had become clogged with motorcars and SUVs and trucks. Information, and other modern, technologies had revolutionised the production processes as human ingenuity, science and technology enhanced the level of development of the means of labour and the productive forces generally.

In Cheddi Jagan's lifetime momentous events left their mark indelibly on him. Much of this story has been told in his insightful book, *The West on Trial: The Fight for Guyana's Freedom*, first published in 1966 with revised editions in 1971 and 1975. Cheddi Jagan's socialisation in colonial British Guiana, his professional training and living as a student in the USA, his embrace of radical ideas and socialism in the 1940s and thereafter, his anti-colonial and anti-imperialist struggles in Guyana and the Caribbean, his political leadership in colonial and independent Guyana, and his political partnership and family life with his dear wife, Janet, have all made him who he was—a political titan.

Cheddi Jagan, throughout his remarkable 79 years on earth, would have been an ear-witness and eye-witness to defining epoch-making events globally, in the Caribbean and Guyana. This 20th century political icon would have been touched by the consequences of the First World War; the rise and fall of the Soviet Union; the emergence and defeat in Europe of Nazism and fascism, the spread of national liberation movements globally, particularly in Africa and Asia, including Vietnam; the Cuban Revolution of 1959 and its full flowering thereafter; the Grenada Revolution of 1979 and its 1983 collapse; the anti-imperialist struggles in Latin America, Africa and Asia; the struggles against racism in the USA and elsewhere, apartheid in South Africa, and Zionism; the processes leading to greater empowerment of women; the struggles globally for equality, justice, freedom and democracy; the founding of the United Nations; and the building of linkages of solidarity between and among socialist countries and non-aligned states.

In the Caribbean, Cheddi Jagan would have been a witness to, and a participant in, the fight against colonialism and for independence, political democracy, and socialism; the controversies and debates surrounding the federal experiment and regional integration; and the building of a political force in Guyana grounded in the working people, the small farmers, and progressive elements of the national bourgeoisie and petit bourgeoisie, including the patriotic professionals and entrepreneurs.

In the process of his political praxis—theory and practice—in Guyana, Cheddi Jagan spearheaded the establishment of the People's Progressive Party (PPP) in 1950; led the PPP in an historic nationalist triumph at the polls in 1953 and then again in 1957 and 1961, and much later in 1992. Sadly, in 1955 the nationalist movement with the PPP as its vanguard was split, a division which manifested itself in a racial bifurcation—Indian and African. Cheddi Jagan and his PPP were removed from office, after 133 days following their 1953 electoral victory, by the British government's ignoble and imperial suspension of the constitution of British Guiana. Consequent upon the PPP's victory at the polls in 1961, American imperialism and British colonialism engineered Jagan's and the PPP's ejection from government through nefarious schemes and machinations on the streets and at the polls in 1964.

Political Philosophy

Cheddi Jagan's perspectives on nationalism, regionalism and internationalism were always grounded in his overall Marxist philosophy. From comparative philosophical enquiry and analysis of the real condition of life, Jagan concluded that dialectical materialism, applied to history, offered the most comprehensive and persuasive explanation of the emergence, sustenance, and evolution or alteration of the various social formations historically. Within those social formations, Jagan accepted, broadly, that socio-political conduct was, and is, determined ultimately by the material order though other factors may preponderate in such determination at various historical moments. Social changes, he insisted, are effected through groups of persons, known as classes, which are defined by their place or role in the social organisation of labour, their commonality of material interest, their consciousness of that commonality and the requirement for collective action. Jagan held to be historically accurate the Marxist formulation that "classes" are the motor force of history by way of their collective actions which are sparked by the contradictions of material life and living, and their on-going resolution in a dialectical manner.

Jagan, like all Marxists, began his analysis from basic concepts which are elaborated into an overarching theory of explanation. At the basic material level there are productive forces which comprise labour (working people), the objects of labour and the means of labour in the productive process. These productive forces plus the relations of production between the various groups in the production process constitute the mode of production. Thus, within the mode of production are to be found "classes" which are the real life manifestation of the relations of production. The mode of production plus the superstructure of ideas, customs, beliefs, laws, and institutions constitute the social formation.

Over time, in history, changes ensue in the respective modes of production through the acting out of the material contradictions located in the particular mode of production. At any one time, there are multiple modes of production coexisting, one of which is dominant and the others are subordinate. A persistent subsidiary mode is that of the small commodity-producing mode of production. The dominant mode of production, according to Jagan, defines the country's or the epoch's social formation and politics.

In Europe, Karl Marx and his intellectual-activist collaborator, Frederick Engels, writing in the mid-and-late-19th century, had posited that the dominant modes of production, in historical sequence, had been primitive communism, slavery, feudalism and capitalism. Each successive mode Marx held to be an advance technologically and materially over its preceding mode. In the case of capitalism, Marx contended that its relations of production, though still exploitative of labour, was the most progressive and advanced in the history of human civilisation. Marx nevertheless predicted that capitalism, as a consequence of its irreconcilable material contradictions resulting in intense class struggles, will be overturned and replaced by a socialist mode of production as a transitional precursor to its full development into communism. Cheddi Jagan was persuaded as being historically correct, the Marxist proposition that the alteration in modes of production occur when the level of the development of the productive forces outstrips, or is inconsistent with, the prevailing relations of production. He was sure that capitalism's demise and its replacement by socialism was inevitable. It was thus the business of his political party, the PPP, to lead the way in Guyana to hasten that inevitability.

Cheddi Jagan and other Caribbean Marxists have understood, in their application of the theses of dialectical and historical materialism, that the historical circumstances of Guyana and the Caribbean did not, in rote fashion, embrace the precise historical sequence of dominant modes of production as Marx detailed in the European context. To begin with, Caribbean societies never experienced a "feudal" mode of production.

Indeed, when Europe was in the throes of establishing a mercantile capitalism, which was later to evolve as industrial capitalism, the Caribbean was still at the stage of "primitive communism" with its indigenous populations of Amerindians, Callinagoes/Garifuna, or Arawaks. European colonialism, with its capitalist economic base, imposed the slave mode of production through the enslavement of Africans in the Caribbean while maintaining exchange relations between Europe and the Caribbean lodged in mercantile capitalism.

Properly-speaking, therefore, the slave mode of production in the Caribbean was technologically more advanced than European slavery ever was, since Caribbean slavery was imposed as an off-spring of European capitalism rather than as a natural outgrowth from primitive communism. The slave mode of production in the Caribbean was peculiarly manifested in the form of a plantation slave economy.

The enslavement of Africans in Guyana and the rest of the Caribbean entwined racism in the plantation economy in that the white Anglo-Saxon plantation slave-owners enslaved black Africans in a European colonial political system which mobilised every specious, and false, justification of the racial superiority of the white European over the black African.

After the abolition of slavery in 1838 in Guyana, and the subsequent importation of Portuguese, Indian and Chinese indentured labourers bolstered, and complicated, the race-class matrices. The legacy of all this still haunts Guyana and its political development.

In *The West on Trial*, Cheddi Jagan devotes a full chapter on "Race, Class, Colour and Religion", although these issues are a constant presence in much of the discourses in his book. Jagan, a finished civilised personality, absolutely devoid of race or colour prejudice, indeed anti-racist to the core, argued thus in *The West on Trial*:

> Race has never been a serious problem. Indians and Africans for many years have played, worked and lived together amicably. Whatever differences existed were mainly economic and vocational....
>
> During the course of our history, there occurred a racial division of labour.... This early division of labour occupationally and geographically according to race tended to prevent integration and to arouse racial hostility. Undercutting of wages of the emancipated Africans by cheap Indian immigrant workers was the source of early conflict. So was the division of plantation labour into 'field' and 'factory'.... The 'mixed' races were the best treated and the best paid, and constituted the bulk of the emerging middle class.
>
> Whatever hostility existed, however, was generally contained except on a few occasions when economic conditions badly deteriorated. "

Jagan further explained:

> In the early period, there were no real conflicts between Africans and Indians; the latter, despised and downtrodden, concentrated on survival. Up to the mid-1920s, they had a

common enemy—the white planters. At that stage, the Indian sugar workers accepted the African militant trade union leader, Hubert N. Critchlow, as their 'Black Crosby'; the class struggle then tended to take on a racial appearance of black against white, and African and Indian against European. It was only when the Indians began to climb out of their 'logie' environment and to compete at the middle-class level for jobs and positions of prestige that conflict began, clearly indicating the economic basis of racism.

Jagan placed the breaking of African-Indian political unity squarely at the feet of the colonial authorities who elaborated a series of political machinations in concert with a section of the local capitalist class and elements within the African and Indian petit bourgeoisie, including some professionals, who feared the class alignment of the working people, drawn from the Indian and African ethnic or cultural groupings, which alignment delivered policies grounded in anti-colonialism, independence, freedom, and socialism.

There are critics of Cheddi Jagan who erroneously caricatured his Marxist ideas as being insufficiently cognisant of race and ethnicity as determinants of socio-political behaviour. These critics contend that he was too slavishly wedded to a crude economic determinism which was at odds with the racial bifurcation in Guyanese society.

I have not seen any persuasive evidence provided by these critics of Cheddi Jagan on this score. Indeed, the analysis which he offers on race, class, ethnicity, and religion demonstrates his profound understanding of these phenomena and their location within Guyana's political economy. Cheddi Jagan's dialectical analysis of these phenomena falls within the frame offered by Frederick Engels in his famous letter to J. Bloch in September 1890. Indeed, Jagan had drawn this very letter to my attention in which Engels expounds on the dialectical interplay between the economic base and the superstructure in the following terms:

According to the materialist conception of history, the *ultimately* determining element in history is the production and reproduction of real life. More than this neither Marx nor I have ever asserted. Hence if somebody twists this into saying that the economic element is the *only* determining one, he transforms that proposition into a meaningless, abstract, senseless phrase. The economic situation is the basis, but the various elements of the superstructure—political forms of the class struggle and its results, to wit: constitutions established by the victorious class after a successful battle, etc., juridical forms, and even the reflexes of all these actual struggles in the brains of the participants, political, juristic, philosophical theories, religious views and their further development into systems of dogmas—also exercise their influence upon the course of historical struggles and in many cases preponderate in determining their form. There is an interaction of all these elements in which, amidst all the endless host of accidents (that is, of things and events whose inner interconnection is so remote or so impossible of proof that we can regard as nonexistent or negligible), the economic movement finally asserts itself as necessary. Otherwise the application of the theory to any period of history would be easier than the solution of a simple equation of the first degree.

And it can be said that Jagan applied the dialectical materialist conception of history to the conditions of Guyana taking into account all the complexities therein. His analysis was not simplistic or mechanistic; it was many-sided, dialectical and materialist, in full realisation of the profound interactions between the economic base and the superstructure.

Nationalism, Regionalism and Internationalism

I shall address Cheddi Jagan's praxis—theory and practice—on nationalism, regionalism and internationalism as parts of a composite whole, which itself is more than the sum of the individual parts. Jagan's praxis on these matters stemmed from his Marxist analysis of society and the necessity and desirability to dismantle capitalism, establish and consolidate Guyana's independence, build regional and internationalist solidarity, and fashion a transition to socialism in the shortest possible time.

In the Epilogue to the 1975 revised edition of *The West on Trial*, Jagan sketched what he called "an all-embracing anti-imperialist, pro-socialist strategy" involving the following:

- Nationalisation of the economy, particularly the large enterprises owned by foreign and local "comprador" capitalists.

- Full democracy and workers' participation and control;

- Genuine diplomatic, economic and cultural relations with the socialist world;

- Training of administrative, diplomatic, technical and professional personnel in socialist states;

- Imbuing the people with revolutionary scientific socialist ideology and involving them meaningfully in the process of socio-economic reconstruction;

- Planned proportional development of the economy with emphasis on industry and agriculture;

- Land reform;

- Strict system of foreign-exchange control;

- Effective rent and price controls;

- Continuing and strengthening of the class struggle;

- Settlement of the border issues so that they cannot be used for launching attacks against Guyana;

- Ending corruption, nepotism and favouritism; fighting and taking strict measures against all forms of racial discrimination, providing special opportunities to all depressed groups, particularly the Amerindians, for development.

Clearly, the economic dimensions of this strategy, particularly those of nationalisation and external economic relations, depended substantially on the existence of a thriving world socialist system headed by the Soviet Union. By 1992, when Jagan and his PPP were re-elected to office after being in the opposition for 28 years, the Soviet Union had collapsed along with the world socialist system. Correspondingly, a triumphalist capitalism and the political hegemony of the USA meant an altered and more accommodating, reformist posture by the PPP in government. Obviously, when the facts change, alterations in one's strategic and tactical approaches necessarily must be altered.

At the same time, Cheddi Jagan never abandoned his quest to build a socialist economy and society. He looked for the requisite spaces, always, in practical terms to pursue this quest in the economy, education, health, housing, the development of the productive forces generally, the construction of a non-racial and more equitable society, the building of democracy and popular participation, regional cooperation, and foreign policy.

From the very beginning of his parliamentary career in 1947, and particularly since the founding of the PPP in 1950, Cheddi Jagan had on the top of his political agenda: anti-colonialism and independence; anti-imperialism; the building of a class conscious working population within the framework of national unity; and the pursuance of a non-capitalist path to development. His objective was to build a genuinely, national, independent, democratic, non-racial, socialist-oriented society.

The respected political scientist Gordon Lewis in *The Growth of the Modern West Indies*, published in 1968, commented astutely on the early years of the nationalist struggle in British Guiana as follows:

> The truth is, indubitably, that 1953 can only be understood in the light of the environmental factors, internal and external, at work at the time. The internal factor was the special character of the PPP. The real offence of Dr Jagan apparently, was that, simply, he meant what he said when, with his colleagues, he declared open war upon the colonial economic-political alliance that dominated the territory.... His was, almost for the first time, the raised voice of the rural disinherited traditionally forgotten by a class of Georgetown politicians, who, as the Waddington Commission of 1951 pointed out, possessed no roots in their constituencies and professed, when elected, little active care for the interests of the constituents. As the new leadership saw the problem, it was open to serious doubts as to whether a colonial instrument like that of the reforms, in which they held the shadow of power while British officialdom held the substance, could either facilitate or permit the fundamental changes they wanted. As indeed, they really did want; this was not a case, Barbados-style, of colonial 'labour' parties using a left-wing phraseology in the service of mild reform....

The PPP, in brief, was interested primarily in the total transfer of power, less so in implementing its reform programme. The British political mind, basically gradualist, could neither understand nor tolerate such an unpardonable violation of its democratic mythology.

The external factor at work was, of course, the climate of international affairs in the 1950s. For Guyana was, in fact the victim of the Cold War....

Imperial culpability, here, is undeniable. Much of 1953 and after was caused by the imperialist need to smash the remarkable unity of the Guyanese African-Indian majority.

...At the same time of course, the disintegration of the popular movement, precipitated by the imperialist interventionism, had its own roots, *sui generis*, in the nature of Guyanese society.

Cheddi Jagan always saw the British suspension of the Constitution of British Guiana as part and parcel of imperialism's world-wide quest in the post-World War II period, to contain or roll back nationalist or socialist-oriented reforms as exemplified in Arbenz's Guatemala and Mossadegh's Iran, among others.

The condition of British Guiana consequent upon the imperial suspension of its constitution prompted the exceptional Guyanese poet of national liberation, Martin Carter, to write in 1954 in his classic "I Come from the Nigger Yard" the following apt words:

> *I come from the nigger yard of yesterday*
> *Leaping from the oppressor's hate*
> *and the scorn of myself.*
> *I come to the world with scars upon my soul*
> *wounds on my body, fury in my hands.*
> *I turn to the histories of men and the lives of the peoples.*

I examine the shower of sparks the wealth of the dreams.
I am pleased with the glories and sad with sorrows
rich with the riches, poor with the loss.
From the nigger year of yesterday I come with my burden.
To the world of to-morrow I turn with my strength.

Despite the arraignment of all the colonial, imperialist, and most of the local capitalist class against Jagan's PPP, it prevailed comfortably in the general elections of 1959 and 1961. After the electoral triumph of 1961, the American government through its Central Intelligence Agency (CIA) in conjunction with British colonialism and local collaborates in Guyana, set about actively to destabilise the PPP government. Their political plots and schemes, including the imposition by the British of proportional representation in the electoral system, conspired to ensure the PPP's defeat at the polls in 1964. The story of all this is well told in *The West on Trial*, in Jagan's parliamentary speeches and in scholarly works such as Stephen Rabe's *Intervention in British Guiana: A Cold War Story*.

Jagan's PPP was to endure opposition for 28 years until their electoral victory in 1992. In 1975, Cheddi Jagan saw the national struggle ahead, thus:

The need is...seen by us for forging a new weapon, better disciplined and ideologically sound party to wage a relentless many-side battle on all fronts—political, ideological, economic, cultural—for genuine independence. Whatever the obstacles, cost and sacrifices, we will continue to work for racial and working class unity and the banner of 'unity and struggle'—struggle against those who vacillate and support imperialism, and unity with those who fight for democracy, freedom and socialism....

Those who say that we are irrelevant, that we are finished, should be reminded that the same tune was sung after the dark days following the rape of our constitution in 1953 and the breakaway by the right and left opportunism in 1955 and 1956. But we won in 1957 and 1961. Today, though defrauded and cheated, we remain the strongest force in the country. Difficulties there will be; the battle will be long and hard. But win again we will.

History and time are on our side.

At the age of 74 years Jagan became President of Guyana in 1992 when the PPP won handsomely free and fair elections. Nearly five years later Cheddi Jagan died. The PPP has then remained in office for nearly 23 years, thus far, under the leadership respectively of Janet Jagan, Bharrat Jagdeo, and Donald Ramoutar.

In Jagan's quest to advance Guyanese nationalism, its development, a spirit of national community, and independence he sought to fashion racial and working class unity in the PPP as the vanguard party of the nationalist struggles. Strictly-speaking, however, the PPP was not a Leninist party akin to the Bolsheviks, later the Communist Party of the Soviet Union. The PPP has never been a narrowly-based party with a membership drawn only from ideologically-grounded Marxist-Leninists. It was decidedly not a party of professional revolutionaries based on the strict criteria of a Leninist vanguard party.

Further, although Cheddi Jagan and several of his principal lieutenants were Marxists, the PPP's leadership circles also contained revolutionary democrats and advanced social democrats who were not Marxists, even though they studied Marxism. The PPP has always been broad-based with a membership committed to independence, democracy, freedom, internationalist solidarity, socialism, and a non-capitalist path to development. To be sure, at various periods in the

PPP's history under Jagan's leadership, the party strengthened its ideological clarity, its organisational bases, and its commitment to democratic centralism.

Cheddi Jagan was always conscious of the necessity and desirability in the circumstances of Guyana to build a broad-based political party, though not a "wash-your-foot-and-come" outfit. Clear criteria for membership were established but Marxist ideological purity was not a pre-requisite although the bulk of the leadership were Marxists who studied and applied Marxism to the conditions of Guyana.

It is important, in my view, to note that Cheddi Jagan, learnt his Marxism in the USA and not the Soviet Union. And he was wedded to the strategic approach of building socialism by way of parliamentary democracy. Interestingly, his profound commitment to parliamentary and participatory democracy placed him at odds with British and American imperialism who paid lip-service to democracy in Guyana but who turned askance against the substance of democracy. Jagan, the Marxist, was the quintessential democrat; the imperialists and colonialists acted in profoundly undemocratic ways.

Cheddi Jagan's principled Marxist formulation of "unity" and "struggle" led him in the late 1970s and 1980s to elaborate the praxis of "critical support" for the Peoples' National Congress (PNC) government of aspects Forbes Burnham's domestic and international agenda which were nationalist and anti-imperialist. Those received Jagan's support; at the same time he critiqued those other dimensions of Burnham's public policies which he considered to be anti-national and too accommodating to imperialism.

Regionally, Jagan was, from the beginning to the end of his life, a staunch defender of the Cuban Revolution. His speeches in and out of Parliament were unequivocal on this point. Examples of all this abound: His parliamentary speech on the "Motion on Timber Concessions to Cuba" on November 4, 1960; his contribution shortly after Guyana's independence in the parliamentary debate on "Foreign Policy"; his presentation in Parliament on "the Sabotage of Cubana Flight 455" on November 24, 1976; and his verbal blasts at the United Nations against the criminal American blockade and subversive activities that were targeted against Fidel and Cuba.

Although Cheddi Jagan saw Guyana as part of a wider Caribbean civilisation, he was, throughout most of his political career, unsupportive of much of what was trumpeted as Caribbean integration. As a Caribbean man, steeped in internationalist, socialist and working people's solidarity, he stood askance against what he saw as window-dressing Caribbean unity which he insisted served the interests of monopoly capital and its political promoters.

His bitter experience taught him that the Caribbean leaders who advocated deeper regional unity either remained silent or sided with British colonialism when the British government, without any reasonable justification, suspended the Constitution of British Guiana and thus removed Jagan's PPP from office in 1953. The only major political party in the region that denounced this subversion of the constitution of British Guiana and the trampling upon the will of the people, was Ebenezer Joshua's People's Political Party (PPP) of St. Vincent.

Unsurprisingly, Cheddi Jagan greeted the West Indies federal venture with extreme scepticism. He advocated a genuine, popular, independent federation, not a colonially-devised structure to set the stage for neo-colonialism.

When Guyana, Barbados, and Antigua and Barbuda unveiled the initiative of the Caribbean Free Trade Area (CARIFTA) in the aftermath of the federation's collapse, Jagan was unimpressed. His contribution to the parliamentary debate on the CARIFTA Agreement on Guyana's Parliament on December 29, 1966, is instructive.

Jagan's position was laid out with crystal clarity:

> We would like to make our position very clear. We say that unity is necessary, but not unity at any price. There are all kinds of unity.... As we see it, this unity which is limited to three relatively small territories will hardly achieve anything, and the unity which is proposed is unity at the trade level more or less in a vacuum, without interfering with the socio-economic structure of these countries; so we have mixed feelings on this whole question....
>
> We do not want to continue to be the importers of manufactured goods and the exporters of raw materials, foods, and minerals. The way to change this is to begin to set up industries, either Government-owned or, according to the philosophy of this Government, private owned! In any case, tariff walls should be put up to give protection to these local industries.... We here are not narrow nationalists, and we do not believe that we must try to solve our problems at the expense of other people. We believe that our nationalism must be tied up with the nationalism of others, but, while we seek unity with other Caribbean countries, we are not prepared to allow our territory to succumb to an inferior status or to see our people relegated to a lower standard of living....
>
> I repeat: We believe in unity, but unity under a set of circumstances which can lead to economic growth and to development, not unity which will allow the foreign capitalists to have a commanding position in the economy of the country and which will allow them to strangle small native enterprises and community enterprises.... Our dilemma on this question is real. We want unity, but we want unity of a special type.

Accordingly, Jagan neither supported nor opposed the motion on CARIFTA. He abstained.

When the PPP returned to office in 1992 with Cheddi Jagan as President, Guyana was already one of the major pillars in the establishment and functioning of CARICOM—the Caribbean Community—within the terms of the Treaty of Chaguaramas of 1973. Work was already well underway for a deepening of regional integration consequent upon the Grand Anse Declaration of 1989. Within four years after Jagan's death, the Revised Treaty of Chaguaramas was signed in July 2001, with the PPP government as a main driver in quest of deeper economic integration of a Single Market and Economy, a more comprehensive package of functional cooperation, and a better regional coordination of foreign policy.

Across the region, Cheddi Jagan actively engaged anti-imperialist, nationalist, and socialist-oriented political parties and organisations. He personally encouraged young political activists and intellectuals to study Marxism; and he participated in leading study sessions. I have personal knowledge and experience of this in Jamaica, Barbados, and St. Vincent and the Grenadines.

Internationally, Jagan's PPP was formally aligned to Communist, Marxist, Socialist, and Revolutionary Democratic political parties. He was the leader of socialism in the Anglophone Caribbean and supported proletarian internationalism, national liberation movements, and anti-imperialism with commitment and a sense of duty.

Jagan's Leadership

Cheddi Jagan was a leader of extraordinary quality. His intellect, his honesty and decency, his humility and calm, his personal charisma, his commitment to the poor and the working people, his promotion of national independence and socialist democracy, and his quintessential humanity, constituted a brightness that sparkled and illuminated; it was never a brightness that blinded. His contribution to Guyana and our Caribbean was immense and towering.

In assessing Jagan's leadership, I consider it apt to quote, at some length, Karl Marx's brilliant work entitled *The Eighteenth Brumaire of Louis Napoleon* published in 1890:

> Men make their own history but they do not make it just as they please; they do not make it under circumstances chosen by themselves, but under circumstances directly encountered, given and transmitted from the past. The tradition of all the dead generations weighs like a nightmare on the brain of the living. And just when they seem engaged in revolutionising themselves and things, in creating something that has never existed, precisely in such periods of revolutionary crisis they anxiously conjure up the spirits of the past to their service and borrow from their names, battle cries and costumes in order to present the new scene of world history in this time.

Leadership is always a complex business, yet in its essence straightforward, though constrained by all the circumstances in which the leader acts. Jagan's essence as a leader was not merely to instil, but to draw out of those whom he led a goodness and nobility which oft-times they did not yet know that they possessed. He had the capacity, almost instinctively, to assess the people's strengths and weaknesses, possibilities and limitations. His leadership task was centred on enhancing the strengths and possibilities and reducing, as far as practicable, the weaknesses and limitations—even to transform these into strengths and possibilities.

I am very pleased that the PPP and the Government of Guyana celebrate, commemorate, and reflect upon the life and work of Cheddi Jagan. I have noted that in several countries of our Caribbean many distinguished former leaders are, in these times of a triumphant neo-colonialism, the objects of mere genuflection as distinct from admiration and genuine love. Some of these former leaders are treated as veritably deranged uncles to be tucked away in the attic of the very house of luxury that many ungrateful successors have inherited. Often, second and third generation successors in politics, the state bureaucracy and the private sector, whose elevation is a direct or indirect consequence of the opportunities created by the former leaders, whisper in embarrassment at the very mention of their path-breaking forbears. These newer arrivants, with such ingratitude, invariably put themselves on an ignoble path of opportunism in the service of a beguiling neo-colonialism. In time they would learn the error of their ways; if they do not, the people would teach them an unforgettable lesson that ingratitude is worse than witchcraft!

Cheddi Jagan's optimism of a better life for the people of Guyana and the Caribbean stemmed not from a sense of the possibilities of divinely-prescribed redemption but from the progressive upliftment of people, ultimately, through their day-to-day struggles of life and living, individually and collectively. This optimism of Cheddi Jagan and his bequest to us have provided the impetus for the fashioning of a comprehensive framework for the study of our political economy and the way forward out of our contemporary travails and challenges.

Sadly, a damning cynicism, encouraged and engendered by imperialism and its globalising chariots, has drained Marxists of redemptive possibilities in our societies. A sterile pragmatism pervades much of the higher echelons of governments, opposition, and universities across our region. Some are afraid even to utter mild formulations such as "social democracy applied to our context". Seemingly, they accept the dominant global political economy as permanent and just, when history instructs us as to its impermanence and its unfairness.

So, I end this evening with a lengthy quotation, touching and concerning, this very issue from a European intellectual transplanted to the USA, Tony Judt, in an essay published in October 2009 and entitled "What is Living and What is Dead in Social Democracy?" Judt offers the following for our reflection:

> Why is it that here in the United States we have such difficulty even *imagining* a different sort of society from the one whose dysfunctions and inequalities trouble us so? We appear to have lost the capacity to question the present, much less offer alternatives to it. Why is it so beyond us to conceive of a different set of arrangements to our common advantage?
>
> Our shortcoming...is discursive. We simply do not know how to talk about these things. To understand why this should be the case, some history is in order: as Keynes once observed, 'A study of the history of opinion is a necessary preliminary to the emancipation of the mind". For the purposes of mental emancipation...I propose that we take a minute to study the history of a prejudice: the universal contemporary resort to 'economism', the invocation of economics in all discussions of public affairs.
>
> For the last thirty years, in much of the English-speaking world...when asking ourselves whether we support a proposal or initiative, we have not asked, is it good or bad? Instead we inquire: is it efficient? Is it productive? Would it benefit gross domestic product? Will it contribute to growth? The propensity to avoid moral considerations, to restrict ourselves to issues of profit and loss—economic questions in the narrowest sense is not an instinctive human condition. It is an acquired taste.

Allied to this narrow arithmetical "economism", is the profound failure of our creative imagination about our possibilities in our region. We have, by and large, not only embraced cynicism as an abiding philosophical premise, we have become wedded to "incrementalism", the handmaiden of a sterile pragmatism. It is widely acknowledged, especially by the cynics, incrementalists, and sterile pragmatists, that the bottlenecks to our region's individual countries' development constitute a virtual chasm. Yet these very people, gripped invariably by a debilitating "learned helplessness", propose the crossing of that chasm in baby steps. But baby steps, metaphorically, would ensure that you plunge ignominiously to the base of the widening gorge. Chasms can only be crossed by leaps. In developmental terms, this means leaps of faith in the people. And that faith must be made perfect, made complete with works.

I have learnt all this and more from Cheddi!

Theology, the Church and Politics: A Caribbean Perspective

(An address delivered at Black Rock, Barbados, on the occasion of the fortieth anniversary of priesthood of the Honourable and Right Reverend Monsignor Vincent Harcourt Blackett, Monday, August 31, 2015.)

Introduction

Thirty-nine years ago, in August 1976, I arrived in Barbados to take up an appointment as a Lecturer in the Department of Government and Sociology, Faculty of Social Sciences, at the University of the West Indies (Cave Hill). I was thirty years of age. I remained in this country continuously for three years until July 1979 when I took a one-year sabbatical to enable me to participate in the first general elections after independence in St. Vincent and the Grenadines that were scheduled for later that year. I never returned to my job at UWI, since in December 1979 the Government of Barbados under Prime Minister "Tom" Adams revoked my work permit on the ground that I was a "security risk". The Government falsely alleged, among other things, that I was "an agent of Cuba and the Soviet Union".

One year before my arrival, on August 15, 1975, Monsignor Blackett, then Father Blackett, was ordained a Roman Catholic priest. After his ordination he was assigned to the Church of Our Lady Queen of the Universe, Black Rock, and Catholic Chaplain to the University of the West Indies (UWI), Cave Hill Campus. I am pleased to be here to be part of the celebration of Monsignor Blackett's fortieth anniversary of his ordination as a priest.

Shortly after my arrival in Barbados, I met Monsignor Blackett. As a Roman Catholic, I attended Mass at the Church here in Black Rock; I partook in Communion. In neither of these religious/spiritual activities did I engage with as much frequency as I would have wished, but I was, and still am, a Christian believer and member of the Roman Catholic Church, although I do not accept every tenet of the organised Catholic Church or every pronouncement of the Pope, Bishop or Priest on this or that social or spiritual issue. Still, I subscribed, then, as I do now, to the core teachings of the church which are reflected in the Bible, the Catechism, the Lord's Prayer, the Credo ("I Believe), and certain fundamental church documents. I emphasise "core teachings", so as to distance myself from a kind of "shopping cart" Catholicism; thus I do not engage in "picking and choosing" this or that as one's fancy directs from a menu of products as if the church were a supermarket. The central joinder of faith and reason is always embraced!

In my three-year stint at Cave Hill, Monsignor Blackett and I became friends; we still are. He was my priest and spiritual adviser. I listened to, and learnt from, his numerous sermons. Over the years I have followed carefully his public statements on a wide range of social, political, and moral issues. I have always considered him to be a holy man of God; a diligent priest in the faithful service of Christ and His Church; a social and cultural activist in the service of his community; a devoted friend of the poor, the vulnerable and the marginalised; a thoughtful theologian; and a human being possessed of grace, exquisite charm, and splendid wit. All of this is wrapped in a folksy Barbadianness lodged within the uplifting ethos of our Caribbean civilisation and the universalism of the Church and humanity.

Let Justice Roll Down as Waters

I believe that it is well-known that while lecturing at UWI between 1976 and 1979 I wrote a column in *The Nation* newspaper in Barbados under the rubric "Straight Talk". I was also quite active as a public intellectual, including as a participant of Monsignor Blackett's Monday Night Forum. I was then, and now, guided in my political activism by the virtues of nationalism, regionalism, internationalism, anti-imperialism, anti-colonialism, popular democracy, socialism, love for people, and an absence of political malice. I was fearless in articulating my opinions, grounded in factual matrices as I knew them.

As a consequence of my political activism and critical commentaries against the then Barbados Labour Party Government of "Tom" Adams, I was traduced on an on-going basis in the news media, on the public platforms, and even in Parliament by defenders of the then government. Among other things, I was threatened with expulsion from Barbados. Part of the standard line against me was that I was a guest in Barbados and should speak not about public affairs in this country; and that I should go back to St. Vincent and the Grenadines from whence I came. Some of the verbal blasts and threats against me were quite hysterical.

In this climate of hostility, Monsignor Blackett sought me out and advised me to read the Book of Amos. He made compelling comparisons with the situation in Barbados and that of Judah and

Israel at the time of the eight-century Prophet, Amos. Monsignor Blackett counselled me to take solace and guidance from the Prophet's teachings.

As students of the Bible know, Amos hailed from the Southern Kingdom (Judah) but was called to prophesy in the Northern Kingdom (Israel) under the kingship of Jeroboam II. The prophetic strictures of Amos roused anger in the hearts and minds of the King. They demanded that Amos go back home from whence he came and that he had no business commenting adversely on the condition in Jeroboam's Kingdom.

What in summary was Amos's critique? First, he declared that the King and his people generally had failed the Law ("the Covenant Code") through a series of specific acts such as abusing the poor, taking advantage of debtors, perverting the course of justice, and acting deceitfully, even on the Sabbath. Secondly, the King and his courtiers had lost all sense of right and wrong, including the commission of veritable war crimes. One commentator, John Bower, in his impressive volume, *The Complete Bible Handbook*, published in 1998, in reflecting generally on the trenchant criticisms by Amos of the ruling elite, wrote:

> They are guilty of inflicting even greater atrocities on their own people. Worst of all, their sin has religious roots, believing their prosperity to be a sign of God's pleasure, without seeing any integral relationship between justice and worship. Self-destruction is inevitable; thus Amos uses shock tactics to shake the people from their complacency.

Monsignor Blackett had drawn to my attention that my political critics, or tormentors in some cases, were mixing blandishments with threats. He had specifically read to me the powerfully principled, prophetic, and poetic words of Amos (Chapter 5, verses 21 – 24) *New International Version* translation:

I hate, I despite your religious feasts;
I cannot stand your assemblies.
Even though you bring me burnt
offerings and grain offerings,
I will not accept them.
Though you bring choice fellowship offerings,
I will have no regard for them.
Away with the noises of your songs!
I will not listen to the music of your harps
But let justice roll on like a river,
righteousness like a never failing stream!

The Prophet Amos is still my guide and inspiration today.

The Priest's Journey

Vincent Harcourt Blackett left school in 1965 and became a Roman Catholic in that very year. In 1968 he entered the Holy Ghost Congregation in Trinidad to begin his preparation for the priesthood.

The 1960s were a time of tremendous change, even upheaval, in the spheres of politics, culture, theology and religion in the Caribbean and globally. At a political level, national liberation struggles and anti-imperialist activism were at the fore in Africa, Asia, Latin America, and the Caribbean. The Civil Rights Movement in the USA and the emergence of "Black Power" in the late 1960s gripped popular consciousness in the Western Hemisphere and internationally. Student protests in cities across the USA, in Paris and Kingston agitated the youths. Popular music by the Beatles, Bob Dylan and then Bob Marley reflected that "the times they were a-changing."

In the Caribbean, the Federation collapsed. Jamaica and Trinidad – Tobago became independent in 1962; Barbados and Guyana followed suit in less than five years. CARIFTA, the fore-runner to CARICOM, was launched in 1965. The University of the West Indies assumed its independence in 1963, having severed its 15-year umbilical links with the University of London. Cuba declared itself "socialist" in 1961. Franz Fanon of Martinique and Algeria caused to be published in 1960 his seminal work, *The Wretched of the Earth;* the New World Movement of Lloyd Best, George Beckford, Norman Girvan and others emerged in the Caribbean, and Walter Rodney, renowned intellectual and activist from Guyana wrote *Groundings With My Brothers,* on the basis of his experiences in Jamaica in 1968.

In 1967, one year before Vincent Harcourt Blackett commenced his priestly initiation, Pope Paul VI published his revolutionary encyclical, *Populorum Progressio.* This important papal document followed upon the path-breaking work of Pope John XXIII's Vatican II convocation of 1962, and following. Liberation theology emerged in Latin America; Afro-centric theological musings arose in the USA; and Caribbean theologians such as Dr William Watty, Dr Kortright Davis, Dr David Mitchell, Dr Roy Neehall, and others, began to fashion a distinctive Caribbean theology through textual interpretations of the Bible in the light of lived experiences in the Caribbean, and to embrace a meaningful ecumenism.

All of these influences, and more, impacted upon young Vincent Harcourt Blackett and helped to shape his consciousness, theology, and priestly journey. The Vatican II Council broke new ground with the *Pastoral Constitution on the Church in the Modern World (Gaudium et Spes).* In the publication entitled *Vatican II: The Essential Texts,* Edward P. Hannenberg, in a commentary on "preparatory material" to the Texts, wrote as follows:

> The Pastoral Constitution on the Church in the Modern World was the only document of Vatican II that was born during the Council itself. Toward the end of the first session—with tensions exposed and frustrations spreading—Cardinal Léon Joseph Suenens rose to address the assembly. He urged his

brother bishops not to let the Council become so preoccupied with the internal affairs of the church that it ignored the rest of the world. The church must reach out and engage pressing questions of social justice, evangelisation, poverty, and peace. He spoke of the need for a triple dialogue: a dialogue among the church's own members, a dialogue with other Christians, and a dialogue with 'the modern world'. His remarks were followed by sustained applause. The next day Cardinal Giovanni Battista Montini, who would soon become Pope Paul VI, endorsed Suenen's proposal. The seeds of *Gaudium et Spes* were planted.

Pope Paul VI's *Populorum Progressio* was a clarion call for social justice, the alleviation of poverty, and peace within the framework of the teachings of Jesus Christ and the Church's historic mission. Indeed, since Pope Leo XIII's encyclical letter *Rerum Novarum* (on Human Labour) in 1891, Catholic Social Teaching had evolved through successive papacies. The theologian, Gregory Heille, OP, in his book *The Preaching of Pope Francis: Missionary Discipleship and the Ministry of the Word* has distilled from this body of Catholic literature the following principles which constitute a cumulative summary framework for Catholic social ethics, as evidenced too in Monsignor Blackett's ministry, namely:

- Every human being is a person, with inalienable rights and corresponding duties.

- Human beings are interdependent.

- The human person is the foundation and end of all human institutions.

- The family is the most autonomous and fundamental human institution.

- State authority properly flows from moral force and the rule of law.

- Intermediate institutions between family and state also serve the common good.

- Human institutions are inter-related according to a principle of subsidiarity.

- The church respects the legitimate autonomy of the democratic order.

- Work is a constitutive dimension of human life.

- The proper subject of work is the human person, not capital.

- Workers have rights to private property, just wages, and to labour unions.

- The common good includes a just distribution of the world's goods/wealth.

- The economic system should allow free work, enterprise and participation.

- Peace is built on a foundation of justice.

- Development is the path to peace.

- The social structures of sin are radically opposed to peace and development.

- Solidarity is the moral response to independence and social sin.

- The church has made a fundamental option on behalf of the poor.

- Social doctrine is a constitutive aspect of the Gospel and evangelisation.

Monsignor Blackett's priestly journey after his ordination in 1975 grounded him in four publics: the Church; the University; the Political Community; and Society. Geographically, his work centred in Barbados but it took him to other Caribbean countries, Latin America, Europe, and Africa. Central to his Ministry have been his Ecumenism, his quest to develop and empower the poor and the marginalised, and his theological praxis between faith, reason and culture. Along the way, Monsignor Blackett inter-faced with titans in the clergy, academia, and society generally, in the Caribbean and globally, who influenced him and whom he undoubtedly touched with his priestly qualities and humane disposition.

In his Homily at the Chrism Mass at the Vatican Basilica on March 28, 2013, Pope Francis addressed, among other things, the issue of "the good priest", as follows:

A good priest can be recognised by the way his people are anointed: this is a clear proof. When our people are anointed with the oil of gladness, it is obvious: for example, when they leave Mass looking as if they have heard good news. Our people like to hear the Gospel preached with 'unction', they like it when the Gospel we preach touches their daily lives, when it runs down like the oil of Aaron to the edges of reality, when it brings light to moments of extreme darkness, to the 'outskirts' where people of faith are most exposed to the onslaught of those who want to tear down their faith. People thank us because they feel that we have prayed over the realities of their everyday lives, their troubles, their joys, their burdens and their hopes…..

We need to 'go out', then, in order to experience our own anointing, its power and its redemptive efficacy: to the 'outskirts' where there is suffering, bloodshed, blindness that longs for sight, and prisoners in thrall to many evil masters. It is not in soul-searching or constant introspection that we encounter the Lord: self-help courses can be useful in life, but to live our priestly life going from one course to another, from one method to another, leads us to become Pelagians and to minimise the power of grace, which comes alive and flourishes to the extent that we, in faith, go out and give ourselves and the Gospel to others, giving what little ointment we have to those who have nothing, nothing at all.

I am sure that Monsignor Blackett's priestly praxis embraces the philosophy and 'modus operandi' of Pope Francis! These are themes or ideas which originate in the Bible. The pinnacle of priestly measurement is that of Jesus the Great High Priest, to which standard mortal priests fall short, but to which they must aspire. This matter is laid out with crystal clarity in Hebrews (Chapter 4, verses 14-15).

Therefore since we have a great high priest who has gone through the heavens, Jesus the Son of God, let us hold firmly to the faith we possess. For we do not have a high priest who is unable to sympathise with our weaknesses, but we have one who has been tempted in every way, just as we are—yet was without sin.

Hebrews (Chapter 5 verses 1-4) further elaborates:

Every high priest is selected from among men and is appointed to represent them in matters related to God, to offer gifts and sacrifices for sins. He is able to deal gently with those who are ignorant and are going astray, since he himself is subject to weakness.... No one takes this honour upon himself, he must be called by God, just as Aaron was.

Monsignor Blackett was selected from among men and was chosen to represent his congregation in matters related to God. I have always had a sense of his divine blessings as one chosen to preach in communion with his people. His authoritative command at the pulpit has always reminded me of God's injunction to Moses at Mount Sinai as told in the Book of Exodus (Chapter 19, Verses 5-6):

> Now if you obey me fully and keep my covenant, then out of all nations you will be my treasured possession. Although the earth is mine, you will be for me a kingdom of priests and a holy nation. These are the words you are to speak to the Israelites.

Monsignor Blackett speaks these words, too, to the Gentiles. One senses that he has adapted the sage advice of the ancient prophet Eli to young Samuel: "Speak Lord, your servant Vincent Harcourt is listening".

A Theology of, and for, the Poor

In his Ministry in the Church and in his engagement with the wider community, Monsignor Blackett has always emphasised a theological praxis of, and for, the poor. The central focus is reflected in the Scriptures.

In his fascinating book entitled *God's Politics: Why the American Right Gets it Wrong and the Left Doesn't Get it* (2005), the internationally-renowned preacher, Jim Wallis, reports on a biblical research exercise as follows:

> We found several thousand verses in the Bible on the poor and God's response to injustice. We found it to be the second most prominent theme in the Hebrew Scriptures Old Testament—the first was idolatry, and the two often were

related. One of every sixteen verses in the New Testament is about the poor or the subject of money (Mammon, as the gospels call it). In the first three (Synoptic) gospels it is one out of ten verses, and in the book of Luke, it is one in seven!

Many persons—some who are on the side of the poor and others who are not—mistakenly take out of context a verse from the *Bible* (Mark, Chapter 14, Verse 7) to justify inaction in addressing the urgent issue of poverty. That verse reads: "The poor you will always have with you." A proper analysis of both the context and text, however, makes the case for solidarity with the poor and the alleviation of poverty.

Mark, Chapter 14, opens with the factual declaration that two days before the Passover and the Feast of the Unleavened Bread, the chief priests and teachers of the law were looking for some sly way to arrest Jesus and kill him. Jesus Himself was, at that time, in Bethany, reclining at the table in the home of a man known as Simon the Leper. While He was there, a woman came with an alabaster jar of very expensive perfume. She broke the jar and poured the perfume on the head of Jesus. Some of those who were present, including presumably some of His disciples, were saying indignantly to one another: 'why this waste of perfume? It could have been sold for more than a year's wages and the money given to the poor.' And they rebuked the woman harshly.

Verses 6-9 of Chapter 14 contain the response of Jesus to all this:

"Leave her alone", said Jesus. "Why are you bothering her? She has done a beautiful thing to me. The poor you will always have with you, and you can help them anytime you want. But you will not always have me. She did what she could. She poured perfume on my body beforehand to prepare for my burial. I tell you the truth, wherever the gospel is preached throughout the world, what she has done will also be told in memory of her".

Then, after this encounter and discussion, Judas Iscariot, one of the Twelve disciples, went to the chief priests to betray Jesus to them.

Several salient facts and circumstances jump out at the reader in this rendering of the Book of Mark (Chapter 14, verses 1-10). The first is that Jesus was at the table of a leper, a poor man and one of society's outcasts. His presence there constitutes a powerful example of identification and solidarity with the poor. Secondly, Jesus rejects the simplistic and abstract approach to addressing the concerns of the poor which was advanced by those who were critical of the lady's use of expensive perfume. Thirdly, Jesus was emphatic in advising the critics that they could themselves help the poor anytime, if they wanted.

In a real sense, Christ's instructive teachings here correspond to, and reflect, the Old Testament commitment in assisting the poor . Thus, in Deuteronomy (Chapter 15, Verses 10-11) it is written:

Give generously to him [the poor brother] and do so without a grudging heart; then because of this the Lord your God will bless you in all your work and in everything you put your hand to.... Therefore I command you to be open-handed toward your brothers and toward the poor and needy in your land.

Fundamentally, the poor and the marginalised are our neighbours as exemplified in the parable of the Good Samaritan as told by Jesus in the Book of Luke (Chapter 10, Verses 24–37). The neighbour was the Samaritan who had mercy on the man who fell into the hands of robbers. Neither the priest nor the Levite, who was untouched and unconcerned about the unfortunate robbery victim, had demonstrated any neighbourly love—"love" the greatest of all gifts according to 1 Corinthians (Chapter 13).

As Prime Minister and Minister of Finance of St. Vincent and the Grenadines, I have always considered that the Annual Estimates of Revenue and Expenditure and the accompanying Appropriation Bill are, among other things, moral documents grounded in the ethical issues of fairness, equity, reasonableness, and faith, which are prominent in Christian theology. Ethics and morality are not mere abstractions but practical lived experiences which connect with reason and a sense of balance. These ideas possess a nexus to expenditure in an effort to lift the quality of people's lives, including poverty reduction, and to revenue, including progressive taxation measures.

On the latter question, an Episcopal layman, William Gates Snr. and a researcher, Chuck Collins, co-authored a probing article entitled "Tax the Rich" in the journal *Sojourners* (January–February 2003). They persuasively argued that:

> Society has an enormous claim upon the fortunes of the wealthy. This is rooted not only in most religious traditions, but also in an honest accounting of society's substantial investment in creating the fertile ground for wealth creation.... Judaism, Christianity, and Islam all affirm the right of individual ownership and private property, but there are moral limits imposed on absolute private ownership of wealth and property. Each tradition affirms that we are not individuals alone but exist in a community—a community that makes claims upon us. The notion that 'it is all mine' is a violation of these teachings and traditions.... Society's claim on the individual accumulated wealth is a fundamentally

American notion, rooted in recognition of society's direct and indirect investment in an individual's success. In other words, we didn't get here on our own.

In the same way in which morality and ethics are not abstractions devoid of practical connectivity, faith is made perfect or complete only by works, by deeds. The Book of James (Chapter 2, Verse 14 et seq.) addresses this issue thus:

> What good is it, my brothers, if a man claims to have faith but has no deeds? Can such faith save him? Suppose a brother or sister is without clothes and daily food. If one of you says to him, 'Go, I wish you well; keep warm and well fed', but does nothing about his physical needs, what good is it? In the same way, faith by itself, if it is not accompanied by action, is dead.... [A] person is justified by what he does and not by faith alone.

Culture and Its Value to Humanity

Monsignor Blackett has repeatedly, over the years, extolled the value of culture to the upliftment of human beings in accordance with God's mission. In an Apostolic Exhortation entitled *Verbum Domini* (The Word of God, 2010), Pope Benedict XVI had this to say on the subject at hand:

> Down the centuries the word of God has inspired different cultures, giving rise to fundamental moral values, outstanding expressions of art and exemplary lifestyles. Hence, in looking to a renewed encounter between the Bible and culture, I wish to reassure all those who are part of the world of culture that they have nothing to fear from openness to God's word, which never destroys true culture, but rather is a constant stimulus to seek ever more appropriate, meaningful and humane forms

of expression. Every authentic culture, if it is to be at the service of humanity, has to be open to transcendence and, in the end, to God.... Sacred scripture contains anthropological and philosophical values that have had a positive influence on humanity as a whole. A sense of the *Bible* as a great code for cultures needs to be fully recovered.

Perceptively, in 1980, in an address to UNESCO, Pope John Paul II commented on this subject thus:

Man lives always according to a culture which is properly his, and which in turn creates among persons a bond which is properly theirs, one which determines the inter-human and social character of human existence.

Monsignor Blackett had long appreciated that "God does not reveal himself in the abstract but by using language, imagery and expressions that are bound to different cultures". As Christianity expands to other cultural milieus, and as cultural alterations or adaptations evolve in established Christian nations, the issues of culture, evangelisation, and the upliftment of human existence intersect with greater force than hitherto.

In the Caribbean, culture and religion/theology manifest several dimensions including: (i) the reflection of God through the cultural prism of our Caribbean civilisation; (ii) the delivery of the teachings of Christianity within a multi-faith context including Islam and Hinduism; (iii) the adoption or adaptation of the form and content of worship; and (iv) the relationship between Afro-centric or indigenous religions, inclusive of their theology and practices, such as Spiritual Baptists or "Shakers" and Rastafarians and more Eurocentric or Americanised religions such as Roman Catholics, Anglicans, Methodists, Pentecostals, Evangelicals, and Seventh Day Adventists.

All these are extant challenges to theology and the religious practice in our Caribbean. Historically, for example Spiritual Baptists were viewed as a 'blot on our civilisation" and were denied their freedom to worship by colonialism with accompanying applause on the sidelines from the leaderships of the established or main-stream churches. Even though the religious liberty of the Spiritual Baptists is no longer curtailed, one senses a lingering prejudice, or more, against them by the major religious denominations. A similar situation, more or less, attends the religious practice of Rastafarians.

The Spiritual Baptist Faith is an African-influenced branch of Protestant Christianity which developed in several countries in the Eastern Caribbean during the 19th Century. The members of the Faith claim lineage from the Biblical fore-runner to Christ, John the Baptist. Many persons who ought to know better continue their disregard, or intolerance, of the Spiritual Baptists on grounds of unacceptable prejudice or considerations of class and Eurocentrism. The central theological tenets and practices of the Spiritual Baptists ought not the invite derision, even if one disagrees with them theologically on any issue. After all, they are Christians. Centrally they practice adult baptism by immersion; mourning as the means of spiritual purification and advancement of Faith; bell-ringing and "shouting" during worship; the visitation of the Holy Spirit while the Pilgrims are in communion with one another and their God the Father, Son, and Holy Ghost; and belief in the complete accuracy and authenticity of the Bible especially the New Testament as the revealed Word of God.

Some other Christians find their "mourning", "bell-ringing" and "shouting" to be unacceptable. I have been advised, however, that "mourning" is justified by reference to the Book of Daniel (Chapter 10, Verses 2-3); "shouting" is endorsed by the prophet Ezra (Chapter 3, verse 11); "bell-ringing" and "visitation of the Holy Spirit" are acknowledged in divers places in the scriptures.

Rastafarianism, or at least one major tendency within it, creates a challenge for other Christian religions on its insistence that the Emperor Haile Selassi Rastafari is a divine being. But mainstream Christian religious are rightly tolerant of Hinduism and Buddhism, for example, with which they disagree profoundly? Why not extend the same religious tolerance to Rastafarianism? Does the explicit African-ness of Ratafarianism create overwhelming difficulties for other mainstream Christian denominations? Is the smoking of "the herb" (marijuana), an illegal substance currently, in the Rastafarians' Tabernacle an unwelcome practice? It would be good to hear from the authoritative voices of the leadership of mainstream Christian churches in the Caribbean on these and related issues. Fundamentally, though, a true ecumenical spirit demands respect and tolerance for all religions under the broad rubric of religious liberty. A recent publication entitled *Exodus! Heirs and Pioneers, Rastafari Return to Ethiopia* authored by Giulia Bonacci and published by UWI Press is helpful in deepening our understanding of the Rastafari Faith.

Faith, Reason, Theology and Politics

Theologians affirm that eschatology is that branch of theology concerned with the final events of history or the ultimate destiny of humanity—"the end times". Fundamentally, as Joseph Ratzinger (Pope Benedict XVI) reminds us in his book, *Church, Ecumenism and Politics* (originally published in 1987; republished in English in 2008):

> Eschatology...is a statement of faith. Based on the confession of the Resurrection of Jesus Christ, it announces the resurrection of the dead, eternal life, and the Kingdom of God.... [Eschatology is] the product of the fusion of Christian faith and the Greek searching for the Logos, that is, for the 'reason of things' that holds them together. It means the effort of thinking through the inner logic of the Christian

dogmas about eternal life, probing this logic from the inner unity of the whole of the Christian message, about God, and man, and thus bringing its content to bear on human thinking in a meaningful way. This quest for a logic of faith allowed the Church Fathers to call faith a philosophy in the sense of a meaningful overview of reality.

Eschatology as a statement of faith is distinct from "utopia". Utopia, as Wilhelm Kamlah instructs us, is "the rational model of the optimal happiness-enabling institutions of a community", which "are proposed as a critique of existing abuses". Thus, as Joseph Ratzinger contends: "Utopia is an appeal to human action guided by practical reason, while eschatology addresses itself to the receptive patience of faith."

The difference between eschatology and utopia would be unbridgeable if faith and reason, receiving and acting were mutually impenetrable. Accordingly, the decisive questions posed and answers given by Ratzinger are:

> Can the eschatological message, which directs men primarily into the passivity of a receiver of gifts, become also a practical statement, one that is oriented to action? And can it engage practical reason? Such a statement that would relegate a human being to the strictest passivity would leave its receiver without any concrete content, it would thereby become meaningless in fact and could not be maintained for long. For this reason if for no other, from the beginning the search was on for a practical meaning of the eschatological proclamation.

In a profound sense, eschatology resides outside of history and utopia is an idealisation of an historical construct. Yet they connect through real human beings possessed of both faith and reason. Through faith, made complete by way of deeds, and rationality, the individual, in Christian collectives, seeks redemption for entry to the Kingdom of God. And the individual acting in concert with, and as part of, civil society, seeks through faith and reason, to improve as best as humanly practicable the condition of the "Earthly City", even as an utopian ideal is posited from the extrapolation of the extant real conditions of life and living.

In the Christian faith, reason comes to light; precisely as faith, it demands reason. And reason comes to light through the Christian faith; reason presupposes the faith as a living space.

In addressing the issues of the "Earthly City" of now, various socio-economic options have been presented historically, including capitalism, socialism, and social democracy within diverse political forms, including, liberal democracy, totalitarianism, and dictatorship. Christian precepts or theological tendencies have been utilised to advance different options and political forms at particular historical periods.

Christians in the "Earthly City", in terms of political participation, have oscillated between positions ranging from "political quietism" at one end of the continuum to "maximalist political activism" at the other end. St. Augustine was, philosophically, a partisan to political quietism, but even he acknowledged that it was impossible in practical terms for this stance to be maintained.

Indeed, practical considerations arise for the people of God even if they are under the yoke of Babylonian captivity. The famous letter of the Prophet Jeremiah (Chapter 29) to the exiles of Babylon is instructive:

> This is what the Lord Almighty, the God of Israel, says to all those who I carried into exile from Jerusalem to Babylon: 'Build houses and settle down; plant gardens and eat what they produce. Marry and have sons and daughters; find wives

for your sons and give your daughters in marriage, so that they too may have sons and daughters. Increase in numbers there; do not decrease. Also seek the peace and prosperity of the city to which I have carried you into exile. Pray to the Lord for it, because if it prospers, you too will prosper.'

Explicitly Jeremiah rejects opposition to King Nebuchadnezzar of Babylon by the exiles. He advises:

The Lord Almighty, the God of Israel, says:

'Do not let the prophets and diviners among you deceive you. Do not listen to the dreams you encourage them to have. They are prophesying lies to you in my name. I have not sent them' declares the Lord.

This is what the Lord says: 'When seventy years are completed for Babylon, I will come to you and fulfil my gracious promise to bring you back to this place. For I know what plans I have for you', declares the Lord.

Among those at the "maximalist political activism" end of the political spectrum are the advocates of "liberation theology", particularly in Latin America in the 1960s to the 1980s and more recently, conservative Evangelism in the USA. Liberation theology sought to blend the redemptive grace of Jesus Christ with the Marxist "prophesy" of a socialist-communist utopia. This fusion created intellectual/theological problems and practical challenges, yet liberation theology was able to evolve a praxis which connected the progressive socio-political consequences of Christ's teachings with the oppression which the poor suffered under monopoly capitalism and authoritarian political over-rule in Latin America. This praxis was elaborated and made manifest in variants of "socialism" in popular democratic forms as evidenced, later, in the experiences of countries such as Brazil, Bolivia, Ecuador, Nicaragua, and Venezuela. Indeed, the "liberation theology" influences, among other things, prompted Michael Manley of Jamaica to declare in 1972 that "Socialism is Christianity in action".

One unintended consequence of the quest for a "new society" as proclaimed by liberation theology, was the equating, wrongly, of freedom or liberation with an absence of obligations to family, the community, the nation, and God. Clearly, the removal of restraints on an individual qua individual without the building of a social individual with bonds of solidarity to others and the community, gives rise to the atomised individual and a selfish, arbitrary individualism devoid of any real appreciation of morality, ethics, and good neighbourliness.

The discourse in the Book of Matthew (Chapter 22, verse 15-21) on the paying of taxes to Caesar is relevant to our reflections on the interface between Christ's teachings and politics. The biblical story is well-known: The Pharisees set to trap Jesus with the query, 'Is it right to pay taxes to Caesar or not'. Jesus, mindful of their hypocrisy, demanded: "Show me the coin used for paying the tax... Whose portrait is this? And whose inscription?" Jesus then made a decisive pronouncement: "Give to Caesar what is Caesar's, and to God what is God's".

This pronouncement or teaching of Christ inaugurated an entirely new era in the history of the relationship between politics and religion. Listen to Joseph Ratzinger on this issue:

> Until then it had generally been thought that the political itself was the sacred...the expression of a sacred, divine, and not merely human will. Because they are divine, they must continue to be untouchable and absolutely obligatory for man.

This equation of the state's claim on men with the sacred claim of the divine will for the world was cut in two by the aforementioned teaching of Jesus.... If Jesus' teaching was true, then the Roman state could not go on as it had hitherto existed. At the same time, it must be said that precisely this division between state and sacred authority, the new dualism that lies therein, represents the source and the abiding basis for the Western idea of freedom.... Where the church itself becomes the state, freedom is gone. But freedom is lacking also in places where the church is abolished as a public and publicly relevant authority, because there again the state claims to be the sole basis for morality.... Where this duality is lacking, totality, that is, the totalitarian system is inevitable.

Monsignor Blackett's commitment to faith and reason and his acceptance of the duality, yet connectedness, between the church and state is the foundation stone for an enduring freedom and democracy in our society as a whole. The link between both signifies an undesirability that neither ought to proceed as though engaged in a suicide pact.

Leadership: A Final Note

It is widely-acknowledged that leadership in any institution, organisation, or society as a whole is extremely important for the success of the entity. There are several dimensions of leadership but I shall touch on only a few for our present purposes, as I conclude on Monsignor Blackett as a leader.

First, the issue of the location of leadership and its scope for action. A leader emerges from his/her specific socio-economic, political, institutional, and cultural context. He/she possesses the possibilities, and is constrained by the limitations, of that context. And great leaders make history, but only to the extent that the circumstances of history permit them so to make.

Secondly, individuals in quest for leadership must be circumspect in balancing ambition and patience. There is an old saying in the Catholic Church that once you sing the choir you can be Pope. But the ambition implicit in that proposition is restrained by the sage advice contained in the hymn that "the good Lord shows His face on he/she who awaits his/her turn". Patience is thus a virtue in this regard; the individual thus waits on the call to leadership. The timely and correct hearing and interpreting the call is vital since many are called but few are chosen. Oft-times ambitious persons mistake a whisper for an unequivocal call. That error can sometimes lead even to tragedy.

Thirdly, the success of someone in a prior job does not mean that he/she would succeed in a higher or leadership post. Some persons are elevated beyond their aptitudes and qualities for leadership.

Fourthly, training for leadership is critical. Invariably the training is a mixture of formal, informal, and experience-based. Daniel's training in Babylon was instructive. The King had caused some of the young Israelites from the royal family and the nobility to be selected for training. The Chief of the King's court was mandated to select, according to the Book of Daniel (Chapter 1):

> Young men without any physical defect, handsome, showing aptitude for every kind of learning, well informed, quick to understand, and qualified to serve in the king's palace. He was to teach them the language and literature of the Babylonians....They were to be trained for three years, and after that they were to enter the king's service.

Matriculation qualifications and training are not 20th century phenomena. Daniel was put into training in the period of Babylonian exile in the sixth century Before Christ!

Fifthly, individuals with "wilderness" experience tend to make better and epoch-making leaders. The "wilderness years"—a metaphoric, not literal expression—clearly seasoned Moses, Joshua, David, the Prophet-Builder Nehemiah, and Paul (servant of the Lord, called to be an Apostle), and prepared them well for their historic missions. Look therefore for leaders who have toiled in the wilderness; those who have been beaten on the anvil of experience and forged in the cauldron of struggle.

Sixthly, the supreme quality of a leader is not merely to inspire his/her following, but to draw out of them that which is good and noble in them; oft-times to draw out goodness and nobility which the followers themselves do not as yet know that they possess. Thus, the leader must correctly assess his/her followers' strengths and possibilities and as far as is humanly possible to transform the weaknesses and limitations into strengths and possibilities. A leader must always eschew "learned helplessness". He/she must be positive and pro-active.

Seventhly, the leader ought to be possessed of, or realistically aspire to the acquisition of, leadership attributes of quality. It is instructive to read the following passage in the Book of Daniel (Chapter 6, verses 1-3):

> It pleased [King} Darius to appoint 120 satraps to rule throughout the kingdom, with three administrators over them, one of whom was Daniel. The satraps were made accountable to them so that the king might not suffer loss. Now Daniel so distinguished himself among the administrators and satraps by his *exceptional qualities* that the king planned to set him over the whole kingdom." (My emphasis.)

Among Daniel's exceptional qualities were his trustworthiness, his incorruptibility and honesty, his diligence, his commitment to service, his vision and creativity, his technical skills, his love of people, and his faith in God.

Monsignor Blackett over his past forty years has displayed true and good leadership in the tradition of Daniel. I have heard him speak of seeking to know himself better; to transcend himself to serve others more wisely and capably; to immerse himself in the complex world around him but not to become worldly; to step back always for daily reflection; to live fully in the present, but also to revere the uplifting traditions of his church and our Caribbean civilisation; and to help in the creation of a better future for humanity at home and abroad.

I thank Monsignor Vincent Harcourt Blackett for his service to God and humanity. I pray for God's continued blessings upon him.

The U.S.–Cuba Accord:
How the Caribbean Paved the Way

(The 17th Eric E. Williams Memorial Lecture delivered at the Florida International University, October 23, 2015.)

Introduction

The sixteen preceding annual Eric E. Williams Memorial Lectures, dating from the inaugural presentation by Dr John Hope Franklin, Professor Emeritus, Duke University, were all delivered by outstanding academics and distinguished political leaders, as befit the memory of the iconic Dr Eric Williams, the towering Caribbean intellectual and political titan, the late Prime Minister of Trinidad and Tobago. I feel truly humbled and honoured to be in the esteemed company of this roll call of invitees who have hitherto delivered the Eric E. Williams Memorial Lecture. Accordingly, I sincerely thank Mrs Erica Williams-Connell; the Eric Williams Memorial Collection Research Library, Archives and Museum; the Florida International University; and all the organisers of this Distinguished Lecture Series.

Permit me at the outset, to affirm yet again that I remain in awe of the sheer intellectual brilliance and monumental achievements which Eric Williams secured on behalf of the people of Trinidad and Tobago and our Caribbean civilisation. I met Eric Williams in spirit and ideas long before I was privileged to meet him personal and direct in early 1969, when I was 22 years of age. My dear mother, who is still alive at 96 years of age, once embarrassed me in an interview she gave to the *Trinidad and Tobago Mirror* newspaper in 2001, shortly after my accession to the Office of the Prime Minister, by recalling that in my early teenage years I would stand in front of the mirror in my room, gesticulating, and imitating the speech and cadences of Eric Williams' voice, as I imagined him in full stride in Parliament or Woodford Square. In those days, Williams' parliamentary and other addresses were broadcast live on "610 Radio Guardian" out of Trinidad. I would listen spellbound, to his voice, reason, and command of language on the old box radio, those with the huge tubes, made by Grundig, a German company.

Later, as a student at the University of the West Indies, I would devour Williams' writings including: The series of monographs from his stint at the Caribbean Commission; the path-breaking *Capitalism and Slavery*; his autobiography, *Inward Hunger*; *British Historians in the West Indies*; *The Economics of Nationhood*; *A History of Trinidad and Tobago*; and numerous pamphlets, including *Massa Day Done*, touching and concerning education, society, and political economy. Subsequently, like all students of Williams, I read with utter amazement his magisterial volume on Caribbean history, *From Columbus to Castro*, written while he was a sitting Prime Minister. The intellectual output of Williams was all absolutely incredible!

In early 1969, I met Dr Williams personally. The occasion was a meeting of the Council of the University of the West Indies—the university's highest decision-making body—held at St. Augustine, Trinidad. Williams was representing Trinidad and Tobago; I was representing the students; I was at that time President of the Guild of Undergraduates, UWI, Mona, Jamaica. Just imagine this: A 22-year old student sitting at the same table with regional political and academic titans such as Eric Williams, discussing the development of tertiary education in the West Indies. During the course of that day, I had the treasured opportunity to speak one-on-one with him. My most favourable predisposition towards him was fortified; I became an admirer, for life!

During my student days at Mona, Jamaica, one of my friends was Patrick Manning, who subsequently became an outstanding political leader of the People's National Movement and Prime Minister of Trinidad and Tobago. I would listen raptly to Patrick's reflections and musings on Williams. Those discussions continued in a more mature fashion during the time Patrick and I served as Prime Ministers. I continue to study the life and work of Eric Williams. And there is some outstanding scholarly work that has been done on him including the contributions by Selwyn Cudjoe, Selwyn Ryan and Colin Palmer. Personally, I consider the best analysis—fair, balanced, well-researched, and insightful—Colin Palmer's book, *Eric Williams and the Making of the Modern Caribbean* who delivered the eighth lecture in this Distinguished Lecture Series in 2006.

But this evening is not the occasion for me to speak about Eric Williams; the People's National Movement (PNM)—the Party which he built; and Williams' immense contribution to our Caribbean civilisation. I affirm, though, that my 47 years as a political activist, my 36 years in electoral politics, my 15 years thus far as Prime Minister, have provided me with a bundle of insights on political praxis in our region to appreciate better the Eric Williams enterprise. Williams remains a teacher and a guide for me, in theory and practice, on our Caribbean political economy. His mind was too subtle and his practical endeavours too nuanced, yet principled, to admit to anyone being his disciple; indeed Williams, contrary to popular thinking, bristled at those who proclaimed discipleship. Notwithstanding the polemical critiques of distinguished scholar-activists like C. L. R. James and Lloyd Best, any objective assessment of Eric Williams must conclude that he undoubtedly has a stellar record of accomplishments in every area of public life. And his PNM, despite its limitations and weaknesses, possesses the phenomenal strengths and possibilities to advance, in our region, a sense of Caribbean nationhood, the upliftment of our Caribbean civilisation, economic development, equity, justice, democracy, and good governance; in short, the Williams' PNM remains in the vanguard of shaping the Caribbean as a modern, vibrant, post-colonial society in the evolving globalised, political architecture. Its recent return to government in Trinidad and Tobago under Prime Minister Dr Keith Rowley, is thus most welcome.

I turn now to embark substantively on our conversation on tonight's subject—the US-Cuba Accord: How the Caribbean Paved the Way.

The Backdrop

On December 17, 2014, the American President Barack Obama, and Cuban President Raul Castro announced the beginning of a process of normalising relations between Cuba and the United States of America (USA). The severe rupturing of hitherto normal relations between these two hemispheric states had initially arisen subsequent to the Cuban Revolution of 1959, and more so after the then Cuban President Fidel Castro had declared in 1961 that Cuba was pursuing a "socialist" path. Meanwhile, from the early years of the Cuban Revolution, the US government hatched and executed a covert and overt policy to topple the revolutionary regime in Cuba. On January 3, 1961, the USA withdrew diplomatic recognition of the Cuban government and closed its embassy in Havana. In April 1961, Cuba successfully resisted the Bay of Pigs invasion led by the American government in concert with Cuban exiles.

By then the American isolation of Cuba was in full swing. Swiftly, the American government imposed a trade and economic embargo on Cuba, cut financial and corresponding banking arrangements, blocked the flow of remittances to Cuba, and sharply restricted the travel of Americans to Cuba. Accompanying all this, was a series of targeted policies and programmes against the Cuban government including political, psychological, propaganda offensives; military and intelligence activities; assassination attempts against the Cuban leadership; and diplomatic measures. At each turn, the Cuban government resisted all these American efforts; instituted counter-measures of one kind or another; deepened and extended its socialist-communist re-ordering of the Cuban society and political economy; waged an anti-imperialist campaign against the USA particularly in Latin America, Africa, Asia, and the Caribbean; cemented its ties with the Soviet Union, and became a member of the so-called "Soviet Bloc"; and, overall, defended the integrity of the Cuban revolutionary process and State.

At the height of the Cold War between the USA and the Soviet Union in the 1960s, no Latin American country save and except Mexico, maintained diplomatic relations with Cuba. At the insistence of the governments of the USA and the vast majority of those of Latin America, Cuba was expelled from the Organisation of American States (OAS).

The collapse of the Soviet Union and its Eastern European allies in the late 1980s to the early 1990s brought an effective end to the Cold War. The impact of the collapse of those regimes, which travelled under the rubric of "international communism", wreaked socio-economic havoc in Cuba. A "special period" was inaugurated as the Cuban Revolution fought for its survival and embarked on a re-arrangement of its emphases in international relations.

The imminent demise of the Cuban Revolution was gleefully predicted in influential circles in government and academia in the USA. Opportunities were thus seized to tighten the screws against Cuba: Legislative measures were passed in the US Congress to fortify American sanctions against Cuba, including through the use of extra-territorial jurisdiction, as manifested in the Cuban Democracy Act of 1992. ("the Toricelli Law"), the Cuban Liberty and Democracy Solidarity Act of 1996 ("the Helms-Burton Act"); US President G. W. Bush's well-funded initiative in 2003 called the Commission for Assistance to a Free Cuba; and the overall political and diplomatic measures devised in accordance with President Bush's declaration in 2004 that Cuba was one of the few "outposts of tyranny" remaining in the world. Indeed, at a CARICOM-USA Summit in 2007 in Washington, co-chaired by President Bush and me, he unambiguously declared that Cuba was a land of "unfreedom" to which the USA was obliged "to deliver freedom". When Fidel Castro resigned as President of Cuba in 2008, the US Deputy Secretary of State, John Negroponte, insisted that the United States would maintain its embargo against Cuba. This policy stance remained in full effect until the Obama "normalisation opening" of December 2014, a composite of piece-meal measures. On July 20, 2015, the United States of America and Cuba restored diplomatic relations which had been severed 54 years earlier. Since then several other ameliorative steps on the normalisation process have been taken by the USA, but the essence of the trade, economic, and financial embargo remains for further legislative and executive action in the USA.

By the time President Obama had elaborated his "normalisation process", most of the world has already determined that American policy in relation to Cuba had failed; indeed, it was viewed globally as a ridiculous anachronism, a relic of the Cold War, and an untenable, unnecessary and undesirable fissure in the hemispheric family. Even the hitherto near-monolithic consensus in the Cuban émigré community in South Florida in favour of isolating the Cuban government had given way to a more nuanced acceptance of a normalisation of relations between the USA and Cuba. Moreover, polling data indicate that a significant majority of Americans were supportive of "normalisation".

The Caribbean Community and Cuba: The Setting

A bundle of circumstances has always pre-disposed and induced the member-states of the Caribbean Community (CARICOM) and Cuba to establish, and nurture, people-to-people links and state-to-state relations, despite the rupture occasioned by Cold War politics in the decade 1962 to 1972. Geographic closeness, European colonisation, ties of commerce and migration, and security considerations prompted and sustained these linkages.

Britain, the colonial power in the Anglophone Caribbean, had friendly relations with pre-revolutionary Cuba in the first half of the 20th century. Citizens of Caribbean countries migrated to Cuba to work in the service industries and on the sugar plantations. Indeed, my paternal grandfather migrated to Cuba from St. Vincent for a two-year period to work as a cane-cuter in Oriente Province during the late 1920s. Santiago de Cuba was heavily populated by Caribbean nationals especially from Jamaica and Haiti. Raul Castro told me three or so years ago that his initial love for Jamaica and Haiti sprang from his interactions as a boy with two migrants from the Caribbean: One, a Jamaican lady, whom his father hired to teach him English— unsuccessfully as it turned out due to Raul's lack of interest at the time; and the second, a Haitian woman, who assisted his mother in the household. The offspring of Caribbean migrants are to be found all over Cuba today, particularly in and around Havana and Santiago de Cuba. The recent liberalisation of Cuba's emigration policies has prompted many of the descendants of these earlier immigrants from the Caribbean to return to the lands of their forebears to live and work. We in St. Vincent and the Grenadines have received dozens of descendants of those great-grandparents and grandparents who had earlier migrated from our country to Cuba. For quite some time now, dating from the 1990s, there have been no visa requirements between Cuba and several CARICOM countries, including St. Vincent and the Grenadines.

Four member-states of CARICOM, namely, Barbados, Guyana, Jamaica, and Trinidad and Tobago established diplomatic relations with Cuba on December 8, 1972, in an independent, sovereign act in the face of strong opposition from their traditional ally, the USA. Jamaica and Trinidad and Tobago, led respectively at the time by Michael Manley and Eric Williams, had become independent nation-states in 1962. Barbados and Guyana, led respectively in 1972 by Errol Barrow and Forbes Burnham, had acceded to independence in 1966. None of these four leaders was a communist; at the same time they were not anti-communist; they were non-communists. Manley and Burnham had declared themselves to be proponents of a particular brand of "socialism"—"democratic socialism" in the case of Manley and "cooperative socialism" in Burnham's. Barrow was a social democrat of the Fabian variety, the principles of which were applied to his country with a common-sense Barbardianness. And Williams was a pragmatist who embraced "the free enterprise" system but who was, at the same time, partisan towards active state ownership of some central parts of the economy. These four leaders, though, were all nationalists and regionalists who saw Cuba as part of the Caribbean family and never subscribed to the isolationist policy of the USA towards Cuba.

An insight into Williams' thinking of the oneness of a Caribbean identity can be gleaned from his address delivered at a Special Convention of his People's National Movement in November 1970 in Chaguaramas, Trinidad, entitled "The Chaguaramas Declaration—Perspective for a New Society". In this comprehensive policy statement delivered in the aftermath of the so-called "February 1970 Revolution", an anti-Williams uprising, Williams affirmed:

> In the age of independence, many of the governments are now actively engaged in the task of nation-building. This simultaneous process is bound to assist in the emergence of both a national and a Caribbean identity, especially if it is accompanied by a greater awareness of the Caribbean past

and by the very real achievement of such great Caribbean leaders as Hatuey in Cuba, Enriquillo in Santo Domingo, Cuffy in Guyana, Toussaint L'Ouverture in Haiti, George William Gordon in Jamaica, José Marti in Cuba, Cipriani and Butler in Trinidad and Tobago. It must also be accompanied by a greater awareness of non-Commonwealth Caribbean literature—for example, Aimé Cesaire in Martinique, Jacques Roumain in Haiti, Nicolas Guillen in Cuba.

Williams envisioned, too, vital economic and political dimensions to this construction of a Caribbean identity. In the same speech, he advised that:

> The Caribbean must look increasingly towards the other countries of the Third World. There is Latin America, which is still struggling for identity and self-realisation. The Caribbean has for far too long been an outsider in the New World and needs to become more closely linked with the other under-privileged countries in the Western Hemisphere …We in the Caribbean and the other peoples of the Third World need each other in respect of markets and in respect of providing a common front against economic domination by the metropolitan countries and in favour of improving the structure of international economic relations to our benefit. These considerations make it imperative for us to maintain and develop diplomatic relations with the countries of Latin America, Africa, and Asia—as we stated quite unambiguously in *The People's Charter* in 1956.

In his book, *Eric Williams and the Making of the Modern Caribbean*, Professor Colin Palmer, renders to us an apt analysis:

> Throughout his career, Eric Williams never wavered from his vision of a politically and economically integrated Anglophone Caribbean. He imagined a closer association

with other countries in the Caribbean but felt that ideally such arrangements would be restricted to those nations that embraced democratic ideals. In the early 1960s Williams was deeply suspicious of Fidel Castro's motives in the region and had little contact with him or his government... Still, by 1964, he was willing to accept Cuba, Haiti, and the Dominican Republic into the larger Caribbean economic union that he was contemplating. Williams envisaged a Caribbean region free from colonial rule, responsible for its own destiny, and integrated, if not politically, at least economically.

Errol Barrow of Barbados, ostensibly the least militantly vocal of the four Caribbean leaders who caused the establishment of diplomatic relations between their countries and Cuba in 1972, made some striking comments on this matter in a conversation I had with him in 1977. He considered it an absurdity for the United States of America to expect that independent Caribbean countries would construct their relations with Cuba—a Caribbean nation—through the prism of super-power vainglory and on the basis of American presidential politics of South Florida—a pointed reference to the political pandering of candidates for the American Presidency to anti-Castro Cuban migrants in and around Miami.

Barrow told me an interesting story about the American government's attempt to have him disinvite the Cuban government to Barbados' independence celebrations in November 1966. The Barbados government had invited, among others, the representatives of both the USA and Cuba to attend the celebration of its attainment of independent nationhood. The US State Department was not pleased. So, an official of the American government, derisively referred to by Barrow as "some 'factotum' of the State Department", informed him that the USA would not send a representative to the celebrations if the invitation to Cuba was not withdrawn. Indignantly, Barrow, an erudite Caribbean man of dignity and aristocratic bearing yet with a common touch, contacted Secretary of State Robert McNamara whom he had known since McNamara's time at the World Bank, and enquired about the descent of "American manners". Barrow was astounded that an invited guest to his metaphoric house could lay down such a rude condition for its attendance. McNamara agreed with Barrow that "good manners" precluded the USA from such diplomatic rudeness. Both Cuba and the USA attended Barbados' independence celebrations; and the world did not come to an end!

Michael Manley of Jamaica and Forbes Burnham were bitingly anti-imperialist and resented any American dictation of their countries' foreign policy. For them, Cuba was a fully-paid up member of our Caribbean civilisation with whom the independent Caribbean nations of our region must, as a matter of principle, establish and strengthen diplomatic, political and economic ties. As far as they were concerned, Cuba's embrace of Marxism-Leninism in its re-ordering of that country's political economy was a matter for the Cuban people and their leaders. They insisted that the principle of non-interference in another country's internal affairs was, in this case, inviolable. They held aloft the Charter of the United Nations as relevant and applicable.

The Praxis of Cuba-Caricom Relations

As the other eight Anglophone Caribbean countries acceded to independence, all of them followed the original four in establishing and building excellent relations with Cuba: Antigua and Barbuda, Bahamas, Belize, the Commonwealth of Dominica, Grenada, St. Kitts and Nevis, St. Lucia, and St. Vincent and the Grenadines. Suriname and Haiti, the two non-Anglophone Caribbean nations with membership in CARICOM, had hitherto established diplomatic relations prior to their membership of that regional body.

Indeed, even prior to the formalisation of diplomatic relations with Cuba by these Caribbean States, the Cuban government acting through one or more of its several agencies established links with civil society organisations. Among other things, Cuban Friendship Societies were formed in all Caribbean countries. And in some countries, including St. Vincent and the Grenadines, the Communist Party of Cuba kept organised links with progressive, nationalist and anti-imperialist political parties or movements in the region.

Every CARICOM member-state has had a diplomatic mission in Cuba for several years now; and Cuba has had, similarly a person of ambassadorial rank at each of its embassies in every Caribbean country. Of other nations, globally, only Brazil and Venezuela have diplomatic missions, physically, in every CARICOM country.

Cuba and CARICOM member-states are closely engaged in bilateral, functional cooperation principally in the areas of education, health, sports, culture, science and technology, energy, disaster preparedness, and regional integration. There have been dramatic examples of this functional cooperation from which CARICOM member-states have benefitted immensely: Thousands of Caribbean students have obtained their university education in Cuba on Cuban scholarships; subsidised tertiary medical care and treatment have been accorded to CARICOM nationals in Cuban hospitals; the Miracle Mission Eye Programme, in conjunction with Venezuela, has seen several thousands of Caribbean nationals, receive surgical treatment on their eyes at Cuban facilities, free of cost; Cuban doctors, nurses, and other professionals in diverse disciplines can be found in most Caribbean countries; and Cuba has assisted immeasurably in disaster preparedness and energy efficiency in several CARICOM countries.

There is, too, a subsisting Trade and Economic Cooperation Agreement between Cuba and CARICOM member-states. However, trade and economic exchanges between them have not increased markedly largely on account of the high cost and limited availability of air and sea transportation, legal and institutional challenges in Cuba, an information deficit on trade and investment opportunities, an insufficiency of credit and finance mechanisms, and the United States' economic embargo against Cuba. There is nevertheless a huge potential for growth in trade inasmuch as the Agreement provides for duty free access, with no customs duties, for 297 products from CARICOM countries and 47 from Cuba.

Cuba-CARICOM cooperation is also evident in the area of tourism. For example, the Issa and Super Clubs hotel chains from Jamaica have invested in hotel development at the exquisite Veradero Beach in Cuba. Functional cooperation further exists through the Caribbean Tourism Organisation.

At the level of political and diplomatic relations, Cuba and the CARICOM member-states have been active members of the Association of Caribbean States (ACS), established in 1994; the Regional Negotiating Machinery (RNM) on trade; the increasingly influential Community of States of Latin America and the Caribbean (CELAC) set up in 2013 and includes all nation-states in the western hemisphere save and except the USA and Canada; and the Group of Latin America (GRULAC) at the United Nations. Many CARICOM member-countries and Cuba have, for several years, been actively participating in the Non-Aligned Movement (NAM) and the Group of 77. So, too, has been their participation in the African, Caribbean and Pacific Group (ACP) which Cuba joined in 2000 and which interfaces structurally with the European Union. Further, six member-countries of CARICOM which constitute the majority of the Organisation of Eastern Caribbean States, namely Antigua and Barbuda, Dominica, Grenada, St. Kitts-Nevis, St. Lucia, and St. Vincent and the Grenadines, are members of the Bolivarian Alternative for Latin America (ALBA) along with Cuba, Venezuela, Ecuador, Bolivia, and Nicaragua. ALBA membership provides these six CARICOM member-states with non-reciprocal "free trade" opportunities and access to loans from the ALBA Bank on very concessional terms.

ALBA, above all else though, is a regional political entity with a particular world view which is often at odds with that of the USA, particularly on hemispheric issues, especially on the complex Cuban question, the defence of sovereignty and independence, and the right of each nation to pursue its own political path in accordance with the principles enshrined in the Charter of the United Nations.

The journey from the establishment of formal diplomatic relations with Cuba by the so-called "Big Four" (Barbados, Guyana, Jamaica, and Trinidad and Tobago) of CARICOM in 1972 to the present time, has been characterised by unevenness, highs and lows, inactivism and spurts of activism, gradualism and courageous leaps, consolidation and expansion. Through it all, we have arrived at very close solidarity ties of friendship between Cuba and CARICOM member-states. Let us sketch some signposts, highlights, and meanderings on this remarkable journey.

Some Signposts and Meanderings of the Cuba-Caricom Nexus

Some three years after the establishment of diplomatic relations between Cuba and CARICOM's "Big Four", a major test arose for CARICOM over the matter of the grant or denial of permission to Cuba for its military planes to re-fuel on their journey to Angola in support of the Popular Movement for the Liberation of Angola (MPLA) and its military wing, the Armed Forces for the Liberation of Angola (FAPLA) led by Augustine Neto, who had led Angola to independence in November 1975. The internal opposition to the MPLA was the National Union for the Total Independence of Angola (UNITA) led by Jonas Savimbi who was supported militarily by the USA and the apartheid regime in South Africa.

At first, Barbados had agreed to the refuelling of the Cuban planes, but under pressure from the American government, Errol Barrow withdrew his permission; he was apparently nervous about the possible adverse impact of such a decision on his country's vital tourism industry. Forbes Burnham of Guyana had no such qualms. Accordingly, his government allowed the refuelling of the Cuban planes en route to Angola despite the personal appeal of US Secretary of State Henry Kissinger not to do so. Burnham stood firm despite American threats of reprisals against Guyana. As far as Burnham was concerned Cuba was, metaphorically, on the side of the angels in fighting to defend Angola's independence and to halt the proxy hegemony of apartheid South Africa. As events unfolded in Angola, South West Africa, and South Africa, Forbes Burnham was vindicated. In fact, much later in 1987/88, at the Battle of Cuito Cuanavale, the Cuban and Angolan armed forces delivered a stinging defeat to UNITA and apartheid South Africa, supported by military hardware and more from the USA, a battle which Nelson Mandela, President of a free South Africa, referred to in a speech in Cuba in 1991 as "marking an important step in the struggle to free the continent and our country of the scourge of apartheid".

A second major test of Cuba-CARICOM relations arose in October 1976 when anti-Castro terrorists blew up a Cubana aircraft bound for Cuba shortly after its take-off from the airport in Barbados. Seventy-seven persons were killed; they were citizens of Cuba, Guyana and North Korea. The anti-Castro hostilities had come directly to us in the region but our countries stood firm with Cuba.

Between March 13, 1979 and October 1983, a third major test emerged for CARICOM in its relations with Cuba in respect of the Grenada Revolution. Grenada had acceded to independence from Britain in 1974; it was the first of the smaller territories in the Anglophone Caribbean to become independent, following upon the so-called "Big Four" between 1962 and 1966. On March 13, 1979, a revolutionary democratic political movement called the New Jewel

Movement (NJM) led by Maurice Bishop overthrew, by revolutionary means, the increasingly autocratic, though democratically-elected, regime of Eric Gairy. It was the first time, since colonial conquest and settlement that a government had come to power in the Anglophone Caribbean other than by the ballot box. The American government, suspicious of the anti-imperialist and socialist-oriented outlook of the NJM and the revolutionary government, withheld its recognition of it. At the same time, the Caribbean led by Burnham's Guyana and Manley's Jamaica swiftly recognised the revolutionary government in Grenada. Cuba followed suit almost immediately. Eventually, the US government fell in line after recognition of the new Grenada government was accorded by Britain, other European countries, and the bulk of nations globally. The OECS and the Eastern Caribbean Currency Union (ECCU) endorsed Grenada's continued membership in them; and Grenada, for its own domestic reasons, pulled out of the Eastern Caribbean Supreme Court and established its own national court system, based on British common law, but with a suspended Constitution, which had a "Bill of Rights". The revolutionary government in Grenada pointedly did not sever ties with the British crown; thus, the Office of the Governor General remained intact, representing the Queen of the United Kingdom as Grenada's titular Head of State. It was a peculiar pragmatic arrangement designed to foster widespread acceptance and to promote a sense of continuity amidst revolutionary change. It was the very occupant of the Office of Governor General, Sir Paul Scoon, who purportedly invited the Reagan administration in the USA to intervene militarily when the Grenada Revolution imploded, through factional in-fighting, in October 1983.

Throughout the short life of the Grenada Revolution, the US government was stridently on the attack against it in divers ways. Meanwhile, CARICOM and the OECS accepted the revolutionary government in Grenada through the embrace of the doctrine of "political pluralism", an expression of the doctrine of non-interference in the internal affairs of a sovereign state. At the same time, Cuba and revolutionary Grenada deepened markedly their relations, including military and security cooperation. Although several more conservative CARICOM governments were uneasy about, or even opposed to, the Grenada Revolution, they all accepted the reality on the ground in Grenada. In any event, across the Caribbean, governments and peoples viewed Grenada as a member of the Caribbean family, and as such deserving of their support and understanding. The US government held no such familial feelings and saw Grenada in puerile ideological terms, through the prism of Cold War politics, as an island outpost of emerging "communism" in league with Cuba and revolutionary Nicaragua under the Sandinistas.

Indeed after the collapse of the Grenada Revolution, the American government elaborated a false narrative about Cuba's support for the extreme left insurgency within the NJM which led to the assassination of Maurice Bishop and the demise of the Revolution. Indeed, Cuba was supportive of Bishop personally and was caught unawares of the "infantile disorder" that had gripped the anti-Bishop faction.

The defeat of the Michael Manley government in Jamaica in 1980 by the decidedly pro-American Jamaica Labour Party under the leadership of Edward Seaga and the collapse of the Grenada Revolution in October 1983, presaged a sea change in Jamaica's hitherto close relations that existed with Cuba during the 1972 to 1980 period. Indeed, Seaga recalled Jamaica's ambassador to Cuba, downgraded Cuba's diplomatic presence in Jamaica, and suspended the functional cooperation arrangements between Jamaica and Cuba. Meanwhile, Jamaica deepened its political and economic arrangements with the USA under the Ronald Reagan administration and entered into a structural adjustment agreement with the International Monetary Fund. The return of Michael Manley's PNP to office in Jamaica in the 1989 to1992 period occasioned a return of a closer Cuba-Jamaica nexus, though not as cozy as the earlier Manley era of 1972 to 1980.

Henceforth, through four succeeding Prime Ministerships from 1992 up to the present, Jamaica has maintained warm and quite friendly relations with Cuba.

Indeed, even after the Jamaica Labour Party's resumption of office in the September 2007 to November 2011 period under Bruce Golding, a former member of Edward Seaga's Cabinet in 1980 to 1989, Jamaica's excellent relations with Cuba were consolidated. In a dramatic move, signally a prompt distancing from Seaga's earlier cooling of ties with Cuba, Golding took nearly half of his Cabinet to Cuba to deepen further the extent of functional cooperation in a range of socio-economic matters.

In the decade or so after the collapse of the Grenada Revolution, the CARICOM member-states' relations with Cuba remained largely formal, save and except in the case of Guyana where the ruling People's National Congress (PNC) of Forbes Burnham and Desmond Hoyte and the opposition People's Progressive Party (PPP) of Cheddi Jagan were always strong advocates of closer relations with Cuba, though Hoyte's PNC (1985-92) was found to be frequently equivocating in the period after Burnham's death. Indeed, in that decade of the early 1980s to early 1990s, in the era of "the Washington Consensus" and the dominant years of the Ronald Reagan–Margaret Thatcher axis, governments more accommodating to American foreign policy and interests came to office across the CARICOM region especially in Dominica, Grenada, Jamaica, St. Kitts-Nevis, St. Lucia, St. Vincent and the Grenadines, and Trinidad and Tobago. In fact, Edward Seaga became the leader of the pro-USA pan-Caribbean political entity known as the Caribbean Democratic Union (CDU), a branch of the International Democratic Union in which the Republican Party in the USA, the Conservative Party in Britain, and the Christian Democrats in Germany were dominant.

Interestingly, in October 1992, the CARICOM member-states were lukewarm to the Cuban-sponsored resolution at the United Nations (UN) General Assembly which called for a condemnation of the American blockade of Cuba. In 1992, this resolution was passed by a vote of 59 to 3 with 71 abstentions, and only Barbados and Jamaica of CARICOM voted with Cuba; the other member-states of CARICOM either abstained or were not present for the voting. However, one year later, in November 1993, the voting pattern of the CARICOM countries on this Cuban resolution had markedly shifted: Ten of the twelve CARICOM states (The Bahamas, Barbados, Belize, Dominica, Guyana, Jamaica, St. Kitts-Nevis, St. Lucia, St. Vincent and the Grenadines, and Trinidad and Tobago) censured Washington's position. They were among 88 countries that voted with Cuba; four were opposed, 57 abstained, and 35 did not vote. In 1993, only Antigua-Barbuda and Grenada stood askance from the CARICOM consensus. Thereafter, CARICOM member-states have remained solid with Cuba on this annual anti-blockade UN resolution.

It is evident that the independent and regionalist spirit of CARICOM member-states in relation to Cuba, reasserted itself in the post-1992 era which saw the crumbling of the Soviet Union, the collapse of centrally-planned regimes in Eastern Europe, and a correspondingly altered foreign policy outreach of Cuba, including in the Caribbean region.

Prior to the unravelling of the "communist" regimes in the Soviet Union and Eastern Europe in the 1989–1992 period, Cuba's foreign policy was focussed on a triad: The "communist" bloc of countries globally; liberation movements world-wide, especially in Africa, and Latin America and the broader-based Non-Aligned Movement. Its relations with CARICOM countries were generally cordial with episodes of closer relations with friendly governments, namely, revolutionary Grenada (1979–1983), Michael Manley's Jamaica (1972–1980), and Forbes Burnham's Guyana (1972–1985). The demise of the Soviet bloc of countries compelled Cuba to alter its foreign policy emphases, including its determined outreach in the CARICOM region where it saw immense potential for enhanced economic cooperation and political linkages within the context of its battle against American hostilities. At the centre of Cuba's outreach to CARICOM member-countries was its determination to demonstrate its principled internationalist solidarity in its immediate geographic neighbourhood.

In an interesting paper authored in 2015 by Dr Jacqueline Laguardia Martinez, a graduate of the University of Havana and a Lecturer at the Institute of International Relations, University of the West Indies, and entitled "Cuba and CARICOM in the Changing Environment", the following observation is made:

> The implosion of the USSR and the European Socialist Bloc altered the World Balance. Cuba faced a severe economic crisis and was compelled to incorporate market mechanisms, receive foreign investors and accept hard currency circulation. The loss of its main international associates forced the island to build new alliances.... The post-Cold War context opened to Cuba the possibility of improving the relationship with the Caribbean. The island, while trying to recover its economy without adopting the neo-liberal recipe, promoted a more active participation in regional fora, especially where the United States did not participate. Since 1992 Cuba has counted on the Caribbean countries for a general condemnation [at the United Nations] of the U.S. Embargo.

One author, H. Michael Erisman of Indiana State University, in a 1994 paper entitled "Evolving Cuban-CARICOM Relations: A Comparative Cost/Benefit Analyses" (presented at the 1994 Annual Conference of the Caribbean Studies Association in Merida, Mexico), labelled the post-1992 Cuban initiative in CARICOM as "a peculiar courtship" to which he contended that CARICOM's response was even "more remarkable". Erisman astutely observes that:

Previously the cultural/ideological differences that distinguished the English-speaking Caribbean from Cuba combined with concern about U.S. vindictiveness would likely have served to thwart any serious engagement. But clearly the phenomenon of the new international political order that has attracted so much attention at the global level has also arrived in the Caribbean, one of its most dramatic manifestations being the willingness of the CARICOM countries to embrace Havana's integration efforts despite Washington's threats of retaliation.

Among Cuba's overtures to CARICOM was its request for an official observer status in this august body. At CARICOM's 13th Heads of Government Conference in Trinidad in June 1992, although Cuba's request was not approved, the Conference of Heads agreed to establish a Joint Commission with Cuba to explore the prospects for greater CARICOM-Cuba cooperation in the areas of trade, developmental programmes, and cultural exchanges. This significant decision was taken despite pressure from the American government to persuade CARICOM to the contrary.

The US government, including the Congress, misread entirely CARICOM's mature, non-ideological embrace of Cuba and the prickly independent spirit of CARICOM's leaders and peoples. The post-Cold War attempts by the American Congress to tighten the screws on Cuba were seen by CARICOM's leadership as crude, misguided, and even insulting to their elemental sense of what was right and wrong. So, when the Torricelli Bill with its extra-territorial trade absurdities against Cuba was passed in Congress, and signed into law by President Clinton, CARICOM member-countries stiffened their resolve. This was perhaps best illustrated by the reaction of Eugenia Charles, Prime Minister of Dominica and an early anti-communist supporter of President Ronald Reagan, who remarked that:

I don't think that the embargo should continue—they should let people trade with Cuba if they want to...

Indeed, Prime Minister Charles insisted that Dominica would trade with Cuba as long as it remained profitable to do so. She bluntly informed the region that:

> The U.S. must realise that we in CARICOM are independent countries and in the same way that they choose their friends, we must be allowed to choose ours.... If they haven't realised that the Cold War is over, we have." (Quoted in *Cuba INFO*, Volume 5, No. 5, April 12, 1993, p.4.)

In 1993, the heavy hand of members of the US Congress and the White House was again rebuffed. This time it concerned CARICOM's decision at its 14th Summit in the Bahamas (July 1993) to accept Cuba's insistence on deleting any reference to democracy, human rights, or any similar pre-condition for cooperation in the draft document of the Cuba-CARICOM Joint Cooperation Commission. The document, which was signed, was modelled on similar CARICOM accords with Mexico and Venezuela in which such matters were not raised or included.

The Clinton administration officials had robustly lobbied the CARICOM Heads of Government Conference in the Bahamas to adopt the American approach of utilising economic levers to compel political concessions from Cuba. These U.S. officials did not succeed. Some members of the U.S. Congress were palpably hysterical in their entreaties to CARICOM. Led by the anti-communist crusader against Cuba, Robert Torricelli (Democrat, New Jersey and Chair of the Foreign Affairs Sub-Committee on Western Hemispheric Affairs), several members of the U.S. House of Representatives sent a letter to CARICOM's leaders threatening to deny their countries any future trade concessions, if they did not rescind their decision to delete the human rights provisions from their agreement with Cuba. The last paragraph of this letter reads as follows:

> We had hoped that it would be possible to construct a free trade area in this hemisphere based on our countries' shared commitment to democratic values. Regrettably, those of us who have promoted this concept in the Congress must now reconsider our support for it. It simply is not possible for us to support the extension of trade benefits to the Caribbean region if we believe that the ultimate beneficiary will be the Cuban dictatorship.

CARICOM stood firm in the face of this thinly-veiled economic blackmail. In a cogent, mature response to the authors of the Torricelli letter, CARICOM's distinguished Secretary General at the time, Dr Edwin Carrington, wrote in his missive of August 19, 1993, in part, as follows:

> The basic relationship which the Caribbean Community and its Member States maintain with Cuba, and which it is not proposed to change, can be viewed in the same light as those which presently exist between Cuba and other hemispheric countries such as Canada and Mexico. CARICOM Heads of Government have noted that Canada is in a Free Trade Area with the United States. Also that Canada, Mexico and the United States propose to launch the North American Free Trade Area (NAFTA) in January 1994. They therefore find it difficult to understand the basis for the concerns that the economic benefits from free trade between the United States and CARICOM will flow through to Cuba from a Technical Cooperation Agreement when that does not occur in other cases.

This very stance was maintained by five nationalist Caribbean nationalist leaders (Cheddi Jagan of Guyana, Erskine Sandiford of Barbados, Patrick Manning of Trinidad-Tobago, P. J. Patterson of Jamaica, and Hubert Ingraham of the Bahamas) in their meeting with President Clinton in Washington on August 30, 1993.

On December 13, 1993, the CARICOM-Joint Cuba Commission was established at an official signing-ceremony in Guyana. The American government, which had invested so much time, energy and resources—political and otherwise—to derail this Cuba-CARICOM agreement had spectacularly failed to do so. CARICOM's fortitude in this matter was grounded in common sense, the interest of the people of Cuba and the Caribbean, and the sensibility of the necessity and desirability of healing the hemispheric fracture with Cuba. The Joint Commission Agreement, renewable every five years, covers a wide range of economic, technological and cultural collaboration, biotechnology, trade, private investment, and tourism. Relevant working groups to implement the Agreement were set up. Subsequently, too, Cuba has signed bilateral Joint Commission Agreements with every CARICOM member-state. These are splendid examples of a mature regionalism.

On the occasion of the 30th anniversary of the establishment of diplomatic relations between Cuba and the so-called "Big Four" of CARICOM, the first of the triennial Cuba-CARICOM Summits convened in Havana, Cuba. Thirteen of the fourteen CARICOM Heads (eleven prime ministers and the presidents of Guyana and Haiti) were present; Suriname was represented by its vice-president. In an article entitled "Cuba, CARICOM Cement Ties" and published in the Guyana Chronicle of December 15, 2002, the late, great Caribbean intellectual Professor Norman Girvan, correctly commented that this inaugural Cuba-CARICOM Summit "marked a new stage in the consolidation of political and economic relations among these fifteen states of the Greater Caribbean region." Henceforth, December 8th has been observed as Cuba-CARICOM Day!

On that occasion in 2002, President Fidel Castro of Cuba declared that with the establishment of diplomatic relations, in December 1972, the four CARICOM countries:

> ...were charting the course for what would later become the foreign policy of the Caribbean community, characterised until today by three main features: independence, courage and concerted action.

On November 30th, 2014, two weeks before the dramatic Obama-Castro announcement on the re-opening of the "normalisation process", the respected European journalist, David Jessop, in an article entitled "Time for a Deeper Cuba-CARICOM Relationship" offered the view that:

> In Washington, it is now accepted at the highest reaches of the Administration that Cuba's reform process is real and that the US approach is outmoded. As one insider noted recently, the intellectual battle in the White House for a change of policy is won; the issue now is about how, when, substance, and deciding whether engagement will be 'Cuba lite' or 'Cuba heavy'.

In April 2015, I was at the table representing St. Vincent and the Grenadines at the historic Summit of the Americas in Panama, which both the President of the United States of America and the President of Cuba attended together for the first time. The USA-Cuba thaw was proceeding, but the core of the economic and financial embargo has remained. President Obama cautiously mapped the path forward and called for changes in Cuba's political set-up; President Raul Castro reciprocated with cautious optimism of the way forward but insisted that Cuba would not alter its political system. So, the unpredictable, though inevitable, process of change has been unleashed; the unfolding is fascinating to watch. Every interested party in this evolving political shake-up, including the member-countries of CARICOM, has to embrace the possibilities therein and avoid the mis-steps or pitfalls that may lie ahead.

No less a personage than the American Vice-President, Joe Biden, has credited CARICOM in pointing the way for political normalisation with Cuba and making the arguments for meaningful engagement. This summary assessment is correct but the reality has been more complex, and the journey more tortuous and complicated. Still, we in CARICOM have been for forty-three years in the vanguard in the western hemisphere in advocating "normalisation" with Cuba.

As Presidents Obama and Castro made their carefully-scripted announcement in December 2014, and before, the Cuban government and the government of St. Vincent and the Grenadines were engaged in mutually beneficial on-going relations but from which my country has been the disproportionate beneficiary. I emphasise two projects—one in health, the other in physical infrastructure—to signal the value of multi-national and people-to-people bonds of friendship. The first is the seamless interaction between health professionals from the USA under the impressive World Pediatric Project, a non-governmental entity based in Virginia and Missouri, and Cuban health professionals under the Integrated Cuban Assistance Programme at my country's premier hospital. The second project relates to the construction of the Argyle International Airport, the largest ever capital project undertaken in St. Vincent and the Grenadines. The international cooperation on this project includes contributions from the governments of Cuba, Venezuela, Taiwan, Trinidad and Tobago, Mexico, Austria, Ghaddafi's Libya, Ahmadinejad's Iran, Georgia, and the State Export Credit Guarantee arrangements of the governments of the USA, Canada, and the United Kingdom. Some 100 Cuban professionals are rendering their services on this vital airport project which is almost completed. All of this occurs within the context of an enabling framework of excellent diplomatic and political relations grounded in the principle of internationalist solidarity. We in the Caribbean have for years been doing sensible, practical things in concert with Cuba while the USA has acted with super-power vainglory and in response to the narrow imperatives of its domestic politics.

At the second Cuba-CARICOM Summit in 2005, President Fidel Castro paid homage to the memory of four titans of the Caribbean (Eric Williams of Trinidad and Tobago, Michael Manley of Jamaica, Errol Barrow of Barbados, and Forbes Burnham of Guyana). Tonight, honour and thanks are accorded especially to the role of Eric Williams without whom the historic opening of the Anglophone Caribbean with Cuba in 1972 would not have occurred. That was the real beginning of the normalisation process with Cuba in the western hemisphere!

Global Insecurity

(Lecture presented to the University College of Cayman Islands as part of its Distinguished Lecture Series on Thursday, June 16, 2016.)

Introduction

Global insecurity is a subject which demands a realistic, not fanciful or normative, assessment. Realism on this matter requires a sober assemblage of the facts; truth emerges from a scientific analysis of the facts which contain many complexities and contradictions. Our enquiry necessarily must be historical, contemporary, and comparative. Global insecurity affecting the international community or significant parts thereof is a condition of disorder ranging from episodic disruptions of established constitutional or legal arrangements and socio-economic upheavals to a vortex of socio-political mayhem and normlessness. Global insecurity often coexists with a measured global orderliness; obvious manifestations of lawlessness and disorder in particular geographic locales often ride in tandem with global order generally. Indeed, some occurrences or initiatives in the political economy, including technological changes, may at one and the same time create insecurity and set the platform for a more secure condition in the evolving social formation.

A realism on this subject leads me to conclude that global insecurity is normal; an absence of global insecurity is abnormal. The critical question therefore is what is the level of global insecurity that is tolerable, and consistent with a level of living that accords with the accepted standards of human civilisation, globally. That very query gives rise to other salient considerations. Indeed, some forms of global insecurity may be necessary, even though not immediately recognized as desirable, by the relevant populations, in order to achieve security and progress. It is part of a complicated historical process.

This issue becomes germane particularly in respect of technological alterations or innovations. The self-styled maverick in the field of information technology, Kevin Kelly, makes the point well in his recent book, *The Inevitable: Understanding the 12 Technological Forces that Will Shape Our Future* (2016):

> I celebrate the never-ending discontentment that technology brings.... This discontent is the trigger for our ingenuity and growth.... When we imagine a better future, we should factor in this constant discomfort....
>
> A world without discomfort is utopia. But it is also stagnant. A world perfectly fair in some dimensions would be horribly unfair in others. A utopia has no problems to solve, but therefore no opportunities either.

So, neither "utopia" nor its opposite "dystopia", are to be seriously entertained as the realised condition for human civilisation. Kelly suggests the alternative "protopia" which is not so much a destination but "a state of becoming", a process in quest of that which is better than what has existed heretofore. "Protopia" signifies a progressive process awash with complications and contradictions.

It is well-nigh impossible to predict accurately, for the future, the precise contours of global insecurity. Still, though, one can be certain that global insecurity will continue so long as the inevitable constant of conflicts or altered/altering relationships within and between groups, classes, and nations, exist. It does not mean, of course, that a veritable Hobbesian state of nature will prevail or evolve in which life generally is nasty, brutish, and short. Indeed, amidst the host of contradictions and challenges, real possibilities exist for the meeting or resolution of any disruptions, conflicts and difficulties, over time. Civilized men and women cannot hold otherwise since the choice is simply between an uplift for civilisation or a descent into barbarism. Regional and international cooperation and the effective roll-out of elemental forms of democratic global governance are modalities to be pursued in the practical embrace of civilisation instead of barbarism. Underpinning this possible architecture of global governance is a requisite of economic advance, social equity, appropriately applied science and technology, and economic democracy for the populations as a whole.

The Context of Insecurity: The Global Political Economy

Global insecurity arises from multiple sources. Among the principal sources are: Contradictions and crises of global capitalism and other extant economic arrangements; economic dominance and resistance; inequality and poverty; adverse climate change and its consequences; the spread of nuclear weapons and the arms race generally; the pursuit of power grounded in ideology; the quest for hegemony based on religion; the turmoil in governance arrangements in several countries, including the clash between "the old order" and rising insurgents as evidenced for example in the so-called "Arab Spring"; the push for territorial aggrandizement; the defence of sovereignty, independence, or territorial integrity; the battle between localism and regionalism, on the one hand, and the forces of globalisation, on the other; problematic demographic trends, including the alterations in the internal composition of populations; the discontents attendant upon the use, misuse, and abuse of modern technology, including information technology; large scale migration, including the upsurge of refugees and asylum seekers; the spread of infectious diseases globally; the perpetration of crimes such as trafficking in illegal drugs and arms, corruption on a grand scale, human trafficking, serious crimes and violence, and money-laundering; and terrorism, domestic and international.

In my conversation with you this evening I shall address these issues in a composite manner while emphasising matters touching on the global economy, inequality, terrorism, technology especially information technology, automation and the workforce, climate change and connected social considerations which fuel global insecurity.

Twenty-five years or so ago, the received wisdom in the citadels of academia and governments in Europe and North America was that the collapse of centrally-planned regimes in the Soviet Union and Eastern Europe would usher in an era of peace and shared prosperity presided over by a Pax Americana with support from allies in Europe and elsewhere. The celebrated American social scientist, Francis Fukuyama, even proclaimed the much-trumpeted triumph of Western liberal democracy and "free enterprise" system over Soviet totalitarianism and "socialism" as "the end of history". Within a short time the very arrogance of such a proclamation ran headlong into the real world in which the presumptive hegemony of a sole superpower, the United States of America, was challenged on several fronts by multi-polar power centres around which clusters of economic and political activities of growing significance were made manifest.

At the level of the global economy, China, India, Russia, Brazil, Japan, South Africa, Mexico, Argentina, Turkey, and Indonesia, along with an expanding European Union, placed severe limits on

America's economic pre-eminence within the context of a rampaging globalization which benefitted American corporations and their shareholders but not necessarily the American people as a whole. In the process, China became the world's second largest economy, within a touching distance of overtaking that of the USA in aggregate terms. By 2012, Brazil had briefly gone past the United Kingdom as the world's sixth largest economy, even though that country has suffered some economic setbacks recently. And India, with its one billion people was racking up rates of economic growth way in excess of the mature developed economies of the USA and Europe. The evolution of the USA in the early 1970s from the status of a substantial creditor nation to that of a hugely debtor economy has prompted economic, monetary, and financial instability on a global scale. The financial crises of September 2008 centred on Wall Street, the financialisation of casino capitalism, and the sub-prime mortgage adventures, swiftly metamorphosed into a global economic depression, the worst for some 80 years since the last catastrophic capitalist implosion of 1929.

Meanwhile, most of the formerly centrally-planned economies in Eastern Europe and Russia are yet to arrive at a settled economic sustainability.

Contributing immensely to this multi-faceted economic meltdown, and its continuance, have been the rise of international terrorism, especially that of Islamic extremism, as manifested in New York City on September 11, 2001; the ill-fated invasions of Afghanistan, Iraq, and Libya by the USA and its allies; the overall political instability in the Middle East (Iran, Israel-Palestine, Syria, religious strife); the territorial land grabs in several regions of the world including in the former European satellite countries of Russia; the unprecedented rise in fuel prices from US $20 per barrel at the turn of the 21st century to US $147 per barrel in July 2008; the relative scarcity of food and consumable water for large sections of the world's population; and the uncertainties attendant upon adverse weather patterns and climate change.

Global Inequality

Globally, socio-economic inequality has fuelled immense discontent in developed, developing, and emerging economies. The Nobel Prize Winner for Economics, Joseph Stiglitz, focused on this subject in respect of the USA in an article in *The Washington Post* (June 22, 2012; republished in his book *The Great Divide* (2016), in the following terms:

> The seriousness of America's growing problem of inequality was highlighted by Federal Reserve data released this month showing the recession's devastating effect on the wealth and income of those at the bottom and in the middle. The decline in median wealth, down almost 40 percent in just three years, wiped out decades of wealth accumulation for most Americans. If the average American had actually shared in the country's seeming prosperity the past two decades, his wealth, instead of stagnating, would have increased by some three-fourths.

Clearly, globalization has produced winners and losers in the income and wealth stakes the world over. There has been an amazing rise in incomes and wealth of the top one percent globally. In many developing and emerging economies such as China, India, Brazil, several other countries of Africa, Asia, Latin America, and the Caribbean, there have been a spurt in the growth of the middle class and a significant reduction in the level of "dirt-poor" poverty. To be sure, this growth in the middle class and the decline of indigence still reflect relatively low incomes compared to those of the average person in the developed world. Still, the globalised economy has left millions of working people in developed countries and sections of the farmers and workers in developing and emerging economies worse off than before. All these shifts in wealth and income have occasioned global instability, conflicts, and protests.

The turmoil in much of America and Europe, including Britain and its imminent Brexit referendum, is connected to this issue of socio-economic equality which is frequently twinned with the influx of refugees and migrants. In a recent book, entitled *Global Inequality: A New Approach for the Age of Globalisation*, the Yugoslav intellectual, Branko Milanovic, trenchantly observed:

> Politicians in the West who pushed for greater reliance on markets in their own economies and the world after the Reagan-Thatcher Revolution could hardly have expected that the much-vaunted globalization would fail to deliver palpable benefits to the majority of their citizens—that is, precisely those whom they were trying to convince of the advantages of neo-liberal policies compared with more protectionist regimes.

The increased concentration of banking and finance capital globally, the financialisation of a veritable "casino capitalism" divorced from real production of goods and essential services, the deregulation and liberalization of money markets, the extraordinarily swift movement of money facilitated by the revolution in information technology, the financing of the global war machine, and self-imposed austerity in public financing by governments under the diktat of the International Monetary Fund and central bankers, have all conspired to establish a troublesome and unhelpful context in the engendering of global instability.

These and related issues were recently addressed in a magnificent book entitled *And the Weak Suffer What They Must? Europe, Austerity, and the Threat to Global Stability* (2016), authored by the celebrated political economist and former Finance Minister of Greece, Yanis Varoufakis. Varoufakis has traced the sources of Europe's economic difficulties to policy decisions from as far back as the American President Richard Nixon's decision in 1971 essentially to dismantle the 1944 Bretton Woods Accords to monopoly capitalism's evolution through financialisation and the bubbles of derivatives, and to the dominant European governments' pursuit of dangerous policies of fiscal austerity in the wrong circumstances thereby disadvantaging the majority of people, and the said governments' embrace of monetary policies to the advantage of the banks.

Varoufakis' diagnosis is sharp and persuasive. His language is robust in describing the extant condition but his faith in a possible redemption is strong, though not perfect. He concludes, in part:

> During the five months in which I took a front-row crash course in Europe's political feuds, I confirmed one thing: a titanic battle is being waged for Europe's integrity and soul, with the forces of reason and humanism losing out, so far, to growing irrationality, authoritarianism, and malice....
>
> False dogmas are condemned; to be found out eventually, in Europe as they were in the Soviet Union and elsewhere. What matters here and now is that they should be found out quickly. For the human toll of this crisis in Europe is too high and has the capacity to reach parts of the planet that do not deserve to suffer as a result of yet another European debacle....
>
> I think we can pull it off. But not without a break from Europe's past and a large democratic stimulus that the fathers of the European Union might have disapproved of.

The range, depth and pace of globalization signal that this process is entering a veritable new age, to which the global strategist Parag Khanna has labelled "hyper-globalisation". This heightened phase of globalisation is "driven by the confluence of strategic ambitions, new technologies, cheap money, and global migration." (See, Parag Khanna: *Connectography: Mapping the Future of Global Civilisation* (2010.)

This enhanced pace of globalisation provides, at one and the same time, opportunities for human advancement and threats with a potential to destabilise national and global communities.

Global Inter-Connectedness

The spread, ease and penetration, globally, of air and sea transport, telecommunications, banking and financial services, automation and robotics, biotechnology, and other assorted forms of applied technology in production, life, and living, have contributed massively to wealth creation and social transformation. In the process the very human existence, society's networks, the social organisation of labour, the institutions of family, school and the church, politics and governance, have been profoundly altered. Much of this has been for the better, and, at the same time, marked dislocations and instability have occurred, in many cases for the worse.

The very technology that has created wealth and enhanced production has also caused retrenchment in jobs in certain areas and closure of particular enterprises and industries. The very technology that has facilitated legitimate businesses and civilised governance has also greased the explosion of money-laundering and terrorism. The spread of information technology has contributed to better informed citizens but at the same time has also made the governance more challenging due to the extensive publication of falsehoods on a continuous basis.

Serious dislocations, and even global instability, that have been engendered through the phenomenal advances in technological shifts or alterations have been universally welcomed. As Kevin Kelly informs us:

Established industries will topple because the old business models no longer work. Entire occupations will disappear, together with some people's livelihoods. New occupations will be born and they will prosper unequally, causing envy and inequality. The continuation and extension of the trends... will challenge current legal assumptions and tread on the edge of the outlaw—a hurdle for law-abiding citizens. By its nature digital network technology rattles international borders because it is borderless. There will be heartbreak, conflict, and confusion in addition to incredible benefits.

In a fascinating book entitled *People Get Ready: The Fight Against a Jobless Economy and a Citizenless Democracy* (2016), the authors, Robert W. McChesney and John Nichols, address this bundle of considerations aptly:

> It is ironic that the digital revolution is central to the jobs crisis, because these same technologies have been roundly heralded heretofore as democratizing agents that shift power from the few to the many. Although we believe it is difficult to exaggerate the value that digital communication has brought to society as a whole, we also believe the evidence is clear that these technologies are not magical; how they are developed owes largely to the political-economic context. They can be forces for surveillance, propaganda, and immiseration as much as tools of liberation.

This process is already quite evident not only in developed and emerging economies but also in developing countries. In the production process itself and in the organisation of economic enterprises broadly, we see the transformation at work. Let us take two examples in the USA, Kodak and American Telegraph and Telephone Corporation (known as AT&T).

Kodak was founded in 1888 and in the pre-digital age became synonymous with affordable cameras and family photography. In due course, it became a company with global reach. In 1988, Kodak employed 145,000. It had a great history; it was innovative in its field and it treated its workers well. But then came the new age of cellphones and instant photo-sharing devices such as Instagram. Kodak became anachronistic. In 2012, Kodak filed for Chapter 11 bankruptcy protection; it was delisted from the New York Stock Exchange on a day when its share value fell to US $0.36 per share. It lost almost its entire workforce; it reorganised, and by 2015 Kodak employed less than five percent of the workers it had 25 years ago.

Meanwhile, as Kodak went into bankruptcy, Instagram, launched in 2010 as a free mobile app, had some 300 million users by 2014, who do all the work of snapping, editing and sharing photos. Instagram has an employed work force of less than twenty persons only. Facebook, founded in 2004, purchased Instagram for US $1 billion in 2012. Facebook itself, a huge entity worth some US $350 billion with a current share value of US $116 per share, a global penetration of massive proportions, and growing as a veritable state without borders, employed as of March 2015, only 10,080 persons, or some 7 percent of the Kodak's employment figure of the 1960s.

In the case of the global telecommunications company, American Telegraph and Telephone Corporation (AT&T), it was in 1964, the USA's most valuable company and was worth then US $267 million in 2015 dollars. In the 1960s, AT&T employed nearly a million persons world-wide. In 2005, AT&T was purchased by Baby Bell SBC Corporation for US $16 billion. In 2015, Google was the USA's second-most valuable company doing much of what AT&T did fifty years earlier, and much, much more. In 2015, Google had a market value in excess of US $430 billion, but employed 55,000 persons or some 7 percent of AT&T's paid workforce in 1964. No wonder, several insightful commentators refer to the current evolution of monopoly capitalism as "capitalism on steroids". Its destabilizing effect on society is real but its possibilities for civilisation's advance are enormous if properly harnessed and subjected to humanity's collective will and benefit.

Automation, the Work Force and Social Organisations

The future of the workforce is likely to undergo immense changes over the next thirty years with profound implications for people's livelihoods, security, and stability. The Ministry of Defence of the United Kingdom government recently published, in 2014, its fifth edition of a document entitled *Strategic Trends Programme: Global Strategic Trends – Out to 2045*. In addressing "Automation and Work", the document states:

> Robots or "unmanned systems"—machines capable of carrying out complex tasks without directly involving a human operator—are likely to be ubiquitous in 2045 as computers are today. Unmanned systems are increasingly likely to replace people in the workplace, carrying out tasks with increased effectiveness and efficiency, while reducing risk to humans. This could ultimately lead to mass unemployment and social unrest. As robots become more lifelike, perhaps capable of appearing to express emotion, interactions with people are likely to become more sophisticated. The increased capability of robots is likely to change the face of warfare, with the possibility that some countries may replace potentially large numbers of soldiers, sailors and airmen with robots by 2045.

More generally, beyond automation of work, society has a social challenge on its hand to adopt to the rapid-changing technologies Kevin Kelly makes the point well:

We are morphing so fast that our ability to invent new things outpaces the rate we can civilise them. These days it takes us a decade after a technology appears to develop a social consensus on what it means and what etiquette we need to tame it.

Technological developments indeed prompt the alteration of authority structures and the establishment of multiple connections in such a way as to limit or undercut the State and its formal institutions. Thus, competing, though unequal, and shifting, points or centres of authority, power or influence are already emerging in, and between, the formal state apparatuses, international and regional organisations or entities, localised communities and cities, corporations of a national, global, and even "stateless" kind, and networked communities in cyberspace. In the process, the internal democratic systems of nation-state are frequently compromised or even undermined by insufficiently democratic governance arrangements in regional and international organisations and trans-national companies, and the relatively unregulated normlessness of the networked communities in cyberspace. So, too, the states that lack democratic governance are being undermined by the other competing points or centres of power, authority, or influence. An ongoing reality of instability thus exists and will intensify; correctives are made in waves but without an arrival of stability, only a to-and-fro, a flux, a composite of enduring, tolerable instability and stability, at best. Clearly the role and functioning of the nation-state is being altered before our very eyes and those alterations will intensify. The old Westphalian nature of a pristine, sovereign state is undergoing fundamental change, but the altered arrangements are yet to be fully fashioned or framed in relation to other centres of authority or power nationally, regionally or globally.

The multiple dimensions of globalisation has made it imperative that alternative modes of organisation and governance must emerge to accommodate the changes in the society, economy, and polity.

Karl Marx famously elaborated the thesis that whenever the level of development of the productive forces (labour, the means of labour, the objects of labour, technology, etc.) in a society outgrows existing production relations of classes or groups in a particular mode of production, the objective situation arises for a fundamental alteration of that mode of production. Clearly, Marx underestimated the extent of capitalism to mutate into diverse forms so as to accommodate or mute, though not necessarily resolve, the contradictions which arise from the developing productive forces and existing production relations; capitalism has changed its form and mode of expression, and this capacity has caused it to avoid the transformation of the capitalist mode of production into a predicted socialist one. But Marx was on to something profound relating to the necessity and desirability of altered production relations to match appropriately the level of the development of the productive forces. Thus, the ongoing quest, in practice, for global capitalism, is manifested in particular countries, to reorganize its production and work apparatuses, including its production relations, so as to sustain itself optimally. Of course, some real flesh-and-blood people are favoured in that reorganization process while others lose out at the work place, in the mode of production itself, and in the social formation, broadly. Great issues are ahead of us to be addressed coordinately, globally, even if their resolution is neither swift nor easy.

Terrorism and Global Instability

It is accepted by all persons who are possessed of "right reason" that terrorism is both a manifestation and a catalyst of modern global instability. Interestingly, the difficulties experienced by the international community to agree upon an accepted definition of terrorism, indicate the very contentious nature of "terrorism" and its effect in fuelling severe global instability.

The most common definition of terrorism includes four basic elements: (i) the use of violence or threat of violence in order to engender a political, religious or ideological change; (ii) its commission by non-state actors or by undercover agents or personnel of one or more of the apparatuses of a State; (iii) its targets in any society are either narrowly or broadly defined; and (iv) it is a crime and a moral wrong.

The terrorism can be either of an international or domestic variety. It is to be noted that it is widely accepted as a principle that violence or threat of violence falls outside the ambit of a defined terrorism in several active scenarios: (i) if there is a declaration of war; (ii) if peace time acts of violence are carried out by a nation-state against another state by established armed units of the State; and (iii) if the acts of violence are in reasonable self-defence. The difficulty is to ground this general principle in agreed factual situations when they arise. Different nations and groups take different stances on the factual matrices. What is "terrorism" for some, is "national liberation" for others!

Still, the international community outlaws certain specific "terrorist acts". And countries the world over have their own definitions of terrorism. In the case of St. Vincent and the Grenadines, in 2002, I piloted a statute through Parliament entitled The United Nations (Anti-Terrorism) Act (Chapter 183 of the Laws of St. Vincent and the Grenadines).

This Act implemented the International Convention for the Suppression of the Financing of Terrorism and to provide for measures to combat terrorism. Section 2 of the Act defines "terrorist act" as meaning: (a) the use or threat of action which constituted an offence, under several named international conventions or protocols touching and concerning aircraft, civil aviation, internationally protected persons, hostages, maritime navigation, and the safety of fixed platforms on the Continental Shelf; and (b) "any other act intended to cause death or serious bodily injury to a civilian, or to any other person not taking an active part in the hostilities in a situation of armed conflict, when the purpose of such act, by its nature or context, is to intimidate a population, or to compel a government or an international organisation to do or to abstain from doing any act."

On the basis of this definition, and other widely-accepted definitions globally, the reprehensible al Qaeda, ISIL, and other such groups are clearly terrorist. Their barbaric campaigns are major threats to global stability.

On June 9, 2016, the 2016 Global Peace Index (GPI) was issued by an international think-tank, the Institute for Economics and Peace (IEP) which established this widely-recognised index in 2007. The 2016 GPI Report highlighted a "historic ten-year deterioration in peace". It assessed that 81 of the countries analysed were more peaceful in 2015 than in 2014, but declines in peacefulness were found in 79 other countries which outweighed the high levels of peacefulness found in most of the world. The IEP found that the Middle East and North Africa (MENA) as "the least peaceful region in the world", due in part, to the civil wars in Yemen, Syria, Libya, and South Sudan, the ongoing international campaign against the Islamic State (IS) group, and a continued rise in terrorism and violent crimes. In the MENA, countries like Kuwait and Qatar were ranked at a high state of peace.

European nations maintained high peace grades; American, Caribbean and Asia Pacific states showed some improvement. Much of Africa, South Asia, Eurasia, and MENA saw deteriorating peace levels in 2015. Iceland, Denmark and Austria scored the highest peace levels; and Iraq, South Sudan and Syria had the lowest peace scores. The USA ranked 103rd out of the 163 countries included in the GPI. The recent senseless massacre in Orlando, Florida, is unlikely to improve the USA's ranking!

The IEP Report found that:

The largest drivers of the international peace decline were political instability and the increase in terrorism across 77 countries. Rising levels of displaced peoples and refugees also reached a 60-year high, and those individuals now account for nearly 1 percent of the global production.

The refugee camps in Kenya, Turkey, Jordan, Lebanon, and in parts of Europe (with refugees from Africa and the Middle East) are examples of continuing global instability.

The Caribbean has long been hailed as a Zone of Peace and of Political Stability despite occasional dissonance or rupture. It is indeed ironic that the Caribbean nation, Cuba, which has suffered most from terrorist attacks in our region, was blacklisted, for purely ideological reasons, by the USA as a state-sponsor of terrorism until April 2015, when the Obama administration removed it from such a dastardly list and hailed Cuba's positive contribution to the peace process between the government of Colombia and the insurgent guerillas in that country. It is encouraging to note that only last week the Cuban and American governments held a constructive dialogue on joint collaboration in fighting terrorism.

It is to be recalled that on October 6, 1976, a Cubana Aircraft, owned by the government of Cuba, was blown out of the sky off the coast of Barbados by two bombs planted by anti-Castro Cuban exiles in league with fellow anti-Castro terrorists from Venezuela and that country's intelligence agency. All 73 passengers on board the aircraft perished; they were mainly Cuban nationals but also nationals from Guyana and North Korea. Not all the perpetrators of this monstrous act of terrorism—the first in our modern Caribbean—have been brought to justice.

The threats to peace and stability in our region flow from money-laundering, drug trafficking, human trafficking, the trafficking in small arms, violent crimes including an increasing number of homicides, and the recruitment of Caribbean nationals to fight battles globally for the Islamic State of Iraq and the Levant (ISIL) and other religious-based terrorist groups. In the latter regard, it was reported last year that approximately 100 Muslims from Trinidad and Tobago had been recruited by ISIL as fighters in Syria.

Clearly, our region has to coordinate its anti-terrorist security activities far more tightly than hitherto, given the global reach of ISIL, al-Qaeda, and other such terrorist networks. Already our state security agencies work in tandem on security issues bilaterally with the governments of the USA, Canada, Britain, France, and Holland and multi-laterally through a host of international security arrangements. Regionally, security is one of the five pillars of the integration movement in CARICOM which coordinates its security initiatives through several agencies. Further, the member-states of the Organisation of Eastern Caribbean States (OECS) and Barbados have a well-functioning regional security mechanism known as the Regional Security System (RSS). Similarly, regional coordination on strategic and tactical initiatives against money-laundering and the financing of terrorism take place through the Financial Action Task Force and the Caribbean Financial Action Task Force and other entities.

The Caribbean needs to strengthen its focused efforts on the safety and security of travel documents (including their source documents); the potential threats to security arising from some "economic citizenship" arrangements; the movement of criminals and suspected terrorists; the security of its sea ports, cruise ship ports, and airports; the challenges of human trafficking, money-laundering, drug trafficking; and the monitoring of recruitment for international terrorism among its nationals.

The Environment, Climate Change and Global Instability

Among the major threats to global stability, now and in the future, is the real possibility of a reduction in the quality of the environment for life and living, and the adverse effects of climate change. Indeed, together they constitute existential challenges to human civilisation particularly to small island developing countries threatened by global warming, coastal erosion, rising sea levels and highly unstable weather systems, and other especially affected countries subject to droughts and desertification.

The global population is likely to grow over the next thirty years from the current 7 billion people to between 8.3 billion and 10.4 billion. Increasing life expectancy, declining levels of child mortality, and continuing elevated birth rates in many developing countries are likely to see the global population increase to some 10 billion by 2045. Clearly, the growth in population would not be evenly spread; it is expected that population growth would be slower in developed countries to the extent of a decline in some. In developing countries rapid population increase and urbanisation are likely to challenge socio-economic and political stability. The internal composition of the populations, with an increase in numbers of the elderly is likely to cause demographic shifts with potentially harsh consequences. Increasingly, more elderly persons remain in employment, narrowing the extent of job opportunities for younger persons unless economic growth and job creation pick up correspondingly.

Over the next 30 years, a growing population will require more food, water, and energy, thus placing a greater pressure on the environment. Conflicts and wars over food, water, and energy are likely; global instability is likely to increase unless ameliorative and even transformational measures are taken. I am not in the grip of a Malthusian doomsday prognosis since it is likely, too, that the increased population, if properly harnessed, and more equitably served, could create or make available, more wealth, food, and energy; technological improvements in concert with a disciplined and smart workforce are likely to bring benefits for life, living, and production. Still, a huge challenge is ahead of us which demands global coordination, including, all things being equal, the facilitation of migration from more highly populated areas to countries with declining productive populations.

The overwhelming consensus among the relevant scientists is that climate change is mainly driven by human-caused greenhouse gas emissions, particularly carbon dioxide (CO_2) from generating power. The developed countries in North America and Europe and emerging economies such as India and China are the major emitters absolutely and on a per-capita basis.

It is estimated that average global temperatures by 2045 are likely to increase by approximately 1.4°c above levels recorded at the end of the 20th century, if all things remain equal. The experts predict that without concerted mitigation efforts, it is unlikely that it will be possible to prevent global average temperatures rising more than 2oC above pre-industrial levels.

Such a rise in average global temperatures would possibly trigger abrupt, tipping point weather events, including the failure of the Indian monsoons, changes in large-scale ocean circulation, substantial melting of the Greenland ice sheet, and the release of large quantities of methane from the ocean floor. Heat waves would intensify and instances of severe drought would increase; at the same time increased rainfall and more frequent and intense storms are likely in some geographic areas; extra-tropical storms will thus move pole-ward. Already much of this has started to occur.

Global sea-levels are likely to rise by between 0.32 and 0.38 metres by 2050, and larger increases are distinctly possible. Currently, between 270 and 310 million people, globally, are at risk of coastal flooding. Without urgent mitigation and adaptation measures, it is estimated that another 100 million or so persons could additionally be at risk to rising sea levels and flooding, three-quarters of them in Asia. Already, severe coastal erosion is severely affecting small island-developing economies and societies, including those in the Caribbean. A tragedy awaits us in the Caribbean and globally if concerted international efforts to reduce harmful climate change and its adverse effects, do not take place urgently and at the level required.

At the same time, the process of desertification marches on. Currently, arid and semi-arid areas cover about 40 percent of the Earth's land surface and are home to over 2 billion people, almost one-third of the world's population. A 2009 study on this matter by Global Humanitarian Forum suggests that another 135 million people are at risk of being displaced by desertification over the next twenty or so years due to water shortages and reduced agricultural output. It is forecast that by 2020, within four years' time, some 60 million people from Sub-Saharan Africa alone are expected to migrate to North Africa and Europe so as to avoid desertification. This number will continue to rise if drastic climate change measures are not taken to mitigate and adapt.

Recently, in December 2015, at the Conference of Parties (COP) 21 in Paris, within the context of the United Nations Framework Convention on Climate Change, the international community agreed on a way forward to take initiatives to reduce greenhouse gas emissions and for resources to be made available for appropriate adaptation and mitigation measures. Progress on these initiatives and measures are urgent and necessary to be pursued, led particularly by the major emitters who possess the resources for the requisite adaptation and mitigation globally. Still, climate change deniers abound in these countries which may hold up vital progress. I note, in passing that St. Vincent and the Grenadines has signed and ratified the recent Paris Accord. Several major emitters, including the USA, are yet to ratify this international climate compact; it is unlikely that the current Congress of the USA would consent to ratification, although the Obama administration has signed the Paris Agreement.

All the adverse climate occurrences, if left unattended, would affect negatively water supply, marine life, biodiversity, and agriculture. Humanitarian disasters await us with all the attendant human suffering, conflicts, and wars. Vitally, these matters are of the highest security concern. Global stability is at real risk.

Social Sectors and Global Insecurity: A Brief Summation

Globalisation, in all its manifestations, has, I reiterate, profound effects on every dimension of life, living, and production. This is very much so in the social sectors including the areas of health, education, urbanisation, transport, information, automation and work, refugees, migration, the crass "financialisation" of citizenship and passports, corruption and money, the role of the state, and citizen security. As always globalisation is a force for good from which we cannot retreat but if it is not subject to democratic regulation and global governance cooperation and coordination it can endanger global and citizen security.

I highlight here for additional commentary two salient issues from the bundle of social sector concerns. The first relates to health; the second concerns refugees, asylum seekers, and internally displaced persons.

Over the past 15 years the world has witnessed the threats to global security and stability arising from infectious diseases moving swiftly across national boundaries. Examples of these diseases include: SARS (a respiratory disease), swine flu, avian flu, Zika, and Ebola which stirred global panic recently. The dangerous spread of HIV/AIDS from the 1980s into early 21st century indicates the threat to global health and security and the necessity for coordinated responses of an urgent and scientific kind.

It has been authoritatively estimated that 70 percent of emerging infections which have occasioned pandemics have originated in animals. This trend is likely to continue over the next 30 years. Given the fact that the time and location of the new infectious or re-emergence of "dormant" infections cannot be accurately forecast, intensified global preparedness and cooperation are, more and more, required to be effected.

Other destabilising health concerns globally include: Chronic non-communicable diseases such as diabetes, hypertension, cancer, and cardiovascular ailments; mental health and dementia; and public health issues relating to climate change, aging, and obesity.

The ravages of wars, home-grown and violent sectarianism or political conflicts, the adverse consequences of climate change, and shortages of vital material resources such as food and water, have in recent years caused an unprecedented upsurge in refugees, asylum seekers, and internally-displaced persons within their own countries. This upsurge has sparked terrible humanitarian disasters, and untold human suffering, and has occasioned growing global insecurity.

The recent publication Global Trends 2015, published through the auspices of the Office of the United Nations High Commissioner for Refugees, has highlighted the extent of this expanding human and security tragedy. Over 65 million people, the largest number for over 100 years, were displaced at the end of 2015, some five million more than in 2014. The details are heart-rending.

Out of a current world population of 7.4 billion persons, one in every 113 persons is thus now either a refugee, or an asylum seeker or internally displaced. In total globally, there are 21.3 million refugees,

3.2 million asylum seekers, and 40.8 million persons internally displaced. Most of the refugees flow from Syria (4.9 million persons), followed by Afghanistan (2.7 million), and Somalia (1.1 million). Colombia is the locale for the most internally-displaced persons (6.9 million), followed by Syria (6.6 million), and Iraq (4.4 million). More than one million refugees and migrants crossed the Mediterranean into Europe in 2015, fleeing from extreme political conflicts, wars, sectarian fighting, and poverty in the Middle East and North Africa.

The data show that 86 percent of the refugees hail from low-and-middle-income countries close to situations of extreme conflict and socio-economic deprivation. Turkey is the largest host country with 2.5 million refugees. And Lebanon has the highest number of refugees-to-population ratio, nearly one refugee for every five citizens. Painfully, children make up 51 percent of refugees globally, frequently separated from their parents.

How can we better cope with the manifold changes and threats to stability? The broad perspective of Robert W. McChesney and John Nichols in *People Get Ready* is instructive:

> If we the people are going to make the future, that is now, our own then we must begin a knowing, conscious fight for shared prosperity, genuine opportunity, and the full realization of the promise of new technologies. That full promise is being denied us at this point in our history. Through that denial, the promise of technology is being turned against us. The oppressive prospects of technology—to spy on us, to profit off our desperation and misery, to make us work harder for less, to control rather than to free us—are only beginning to be realized....

But this oppression is not inevitable. As McChesney and Nichols further hopefully and persuasively lay out:

174

The future that is next can be good, and it can get better. Dramatically better—for people around the world. Technology can help us to be happier, healthier, freer, and more connected to ourselves, our families, and our communities. We can work less and enjoy our lives more. The tech utopian promise is real.

But there is no gadget that can get society from here to there. There is no app that will achieve the better and more humane life that is possible. There is no master plan from a CEO or Silicon Valley visionary. There is only us. We the people are the only force that can make a future worthy of our hopes and our humanity. And our only tool is that which has ever taken the power to define the future away from the elites and given it to the whole of humanity: democracy.

This democracy, I aver, is both political and economic in nature. Optimal governance and material bases of democracy are requisites for a full realization of the best in organized human civilisation. This is an historic venture for all peoples globally. It is not a call for global governance. It is for political and economic democracy in nation-states (the people, communities, companies, etc.) and their interconnectedness globally through regional and international organisations, and a proper productive and democratic relationship between those elements which are local, national, regional, and global. The global challenges which give rise to instability cannot be tackled only locally or nationally, but the local and the national cannot be sacrificed upon the altar of regional and international behemoths which lack the requisite responsiveness and responsibility. There has to be a dialectical, and uplifting, connection between the local, national, regional, and international dimensions of our human civilisation.

Admittedly, it is a complex governance and managerial architecture to devise for the altered circumstances of the brave, new world. But, as always, divine inspiration, human intelligence, and the people will lead us to success. We cannot and must not succumb to pessimism and learned helplessness; we must own our present and our future!